*Weighing up the Evidence*

HOW AND WHY:

# The English Civil War

Alan Dures

Dryad Press Limited London

# Contents

ACKNOWLEDGMENTS
The author and publishers thank the following for their kind permission to reproduce copyright illustrations: The Trustees of the British Museum, pages 5, 48; Mary Evans Picture Library, pages 8, 10, 16, 17, 19, 22, 27, 28, 32, 33, 37, 39, 41, 47, 50, 52, 54, 58. The maps on page 7 were drawn by R.F. Brien.
   The colour picture on the front cover shows Prince Rupert at Edgehill, 1642. The black and white pictures show Charles I raising his standard at Nottingham, and the execution of the King. (All cover pictures from Mary Evans Picture Library)

© Alan Dures 1987    First published 1987
Typeset by Tek-Art Ltd, Kent
and printed in Great Britain by R J Acford Ltd, Chichester, Sussex
for the Publishers, Dryad Press Limited,
8 Cavendish Square, London W1M 0AJ

# Introduction

On 22 August 1642 King Charles I unfurled the royal standard at Nottingham, formally declaring war against his opponents in Parliament. The English Civil War had begun. For the next three years, Parliamentary and Royalist forces faced each other on various battlefields. By 1645 the Royalist position was weak, but not altogether desperate. But on 14 June, at Naseby, the King's infantry was scattered, his guns destroyed and his baggage train taken. Parliament's New Model Army had triumphed. It triumphed again when it tore to pieces the last Royalist army, led by Goring, at Langport near Bridgwater on 10 July 1645. This was the last pitched battle of the Civil War.

Oliver Cromwell, who by 1645 was in charge of the New Model Army, wrote after the battle: "God will go on", meaning that the Parliamentary cause would continue to progress. And continue it did. By March 1646 the last Royalist resistance had collapsed. However, Charles refused to accept the terms put to him by Parliament. Instead the King tried to exploit the divisions that were emerging on the Parliamentary side. By 1648, with support from Scotland, he was able to make another military challenge against Parliament. He lost again. In January 1649 the unthinkable happened: the English King was executed.

There is agreement among historians that these events took place. What caused the events, however, has been a matter of controversy from the mid-seventeenth century onwards. The purpose of this book is to introduce you to a wide variety of evidence which should show you how and why historians have reached different conclusions about the English Civil War. It should help you to assess critically both contemporary and later sources and thereby enable you to make your own judgements about these momentous events.

Such a task is not easy. Dame Veronica Wedgwood, writing in 1955, said that we are so involved in the issues that we cannot make objective judgements:

The final, dispassionate, authoritative history of the Civil War cannot be written until the problems have ceased to matter; by that time it will not be worth writing.

(*Source:* C.V. Wedgwood, *The King's Peace 1637-41*, Collins, 1955)

There is another problem facing you as well. You need to make an imaginative leap to get inside the minds of seventeenth-century people and to appreciate their way of life. Many values were different from our own. Religion generated tremendous passions: people died for it in this period. Of course it is worth remembering that the same is true of certain countries today. Parliament is now the centre of politics in Britain, and although we have a monarch, she is not involved in everyday government. In the seventeenth century the monarch was thought to be appointed by God and he was the effective ruler of the country. Parliament was called only when it suited the King, so its importance was limited. You need to understand and discuss why seventeenth-century people held such values.

Despite the warning by C.V. Wedgwood, historians since the seventeenth century have tried to discover the causes of the Civil War. There have always been two major points of disagreement. Firstly, historians have disagreed about how far back we must seek for the origins of the war. Was Civil War inevitable by the early seventeenth century because of social, political and religious changes in the sixteenth century? Or was it, at the other extreme, only the events of 1640-42 that plunged the country into turmoil? Secondly, there has always been dispute over the issues that drove Englishmen to war: was it religion or politics, or even the personal incompetence of Charles I?

The Earl of Clarendon, in his *History of the Rebellion and Civil Wars in England*, begun in 1646, thought that short-term explanations were sufficient:

I shall not lead any man farther back in this journey, for the discovery of the entrance into these dark ways than the beginning of this king's [Charles I's] reign. For I am not so sharp-sighted as those, who have discerned this rebellion contriving from (if not before) the death of Queen Elizabeth. . . . Neither do I look so far back as believing the design to be so long since formed.

James Harrington believed that long-term social changes, especially the decline of the aristocracy, led to the Civil War. In 1656 Harrington wrote a book explaining these ideas but, like a number of writers before him, he put them in the form of a story about what happened to an imaginary state called Oceana:

The dissolution of the late monarchy was as natural as the death of a man. . . . Oceana, or any other nation of no greater extent must have a competent nobility, or is altogether incapable of monarchy. . .

(*Source: The Commonwealth of Oceana*, 1656)

The debate about whether the Civil War should be explained by long- or short-term factors continues with modern historians. In a recent publication, Christopher Hill summed up his views and others':

H.R. Trevor-Roper thinks there were no problems in 1641 which could not have been solved by sensible men sitting around a table. Lawrence Stone regards the English Revolution as one of the great revolutions of history, comparable with the American, French and Russian Revolutions. F.J. Fisher, on the contrary, says the Civil War was "the result of the breakdown of a clumsy political machine in the hands of a remarkably inefficient operator." On this point I agree with Stone and disagree with Trevor-Roper and Fisher.

(*Source:* C. Hill, *A Society Divided*, Open University, Block 3, A203 Course, 1980)

As to the actual issues, contemporaries stress three causes: religion, especially the challenge of the Puritans, who wanted to change the Anglican Church; the political contest between Crown and Parliament; and the personal deficiencies of the King. Puritanism led Simon D'Ewes, an important Parliamentarian and famous diarist, to "oppose the King". He supported Parliament

> so that religion might be established in that power and purity among us, and preaching so settled in those places where atheism, profaneness and ignorance now reigns.
>
> (*Source: Seventeenth Century England: A Changing Culture*, Vol. 1, Primary Sources, ed. Ann Hughes, Open University, 1980)

Richard Baxter, a chaplain to the Parliamentary Army, believed that the Royalists consisted mainly of those who were anti-Puritan:

> The Gentry [who supported the King] were not so precise and strict against an Oath or Gaming, or Plays or Drinking, nor troubled themselves so much about the Matters of God and the World to come . . . and [those that were glad] to hear a sermon which lasht the Puritans . . . the main body of these were against the parliament.
>
> (*Source: Seventeenth Century England: A Changing Culture*)

Thomas Hobbes, a famous political theorist, saw the issue as a political

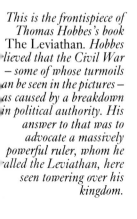

*This is the frontispiece of Thomas Hobbes's book* The Leviathan. *Hobbes believed that the Civil War – some of whose turmoils can be seen in the pictures – was caused by a breakdown in political authority. His answer to that was to advocate a massively powerful ruler, whom he called the Leviathan, here seen towering over his kingdom.*

one. The King had lost power because the people had been given too much freedom and Parliament had challenged the King.

The core of the rebellion . . . are the universities which nevertheless are not to be cast away, but to be better disciplined; that is to say that politics there taught be made to be (as true politics should be) such as are fit to make men know that it is their duty to obey all laws whatsoever that shall by the authority of the king be enacted.

(*Source:* Thomas Hobbes, *Behemoth*, 1679)

But for Thomas May it was Charles I's oppressive policies that caused the Civil War. Thomas May was one of the first people to write about the Civil War in a publication of 1650.

Forty years old was King Charles and fifteen years had he reigned when this Parliament was called [i.e. in 1640]: so long had the laws been violated, the liberties of the people invaded and the authority of Parliament, by which laws and liberties are supported, trodden under foot: which had by degrees much discontented the English nation.

(*Source: A Breviary of the History of the Parliament of England*, 1650)

Historians today still differ about which was the most important issue in bringing about the Civil War. Some, such as Christopher Hill, emphasize the significance of economic factors and claim that there were class differences between the two sides. Some historians see the main point as the opposition to a potentially tyrannical king; Parliament was protecting the "liberties" and freedoms of the subject. In more recent years, however, religion has been picked out once again as the key issue in causing people to go to war (see page 56).

We begin our examination of the possible causes of the Civil War in the sixteenth century. You need to be clear about the exact events you are analysing. The main aim is to find out why the Civil War broke out in 1642, but the book goes on beyond that point and asks you to investigate why the whole episode ended with the execution of King Charles I, when no one in 1642 envisaged such an outcome. The aim of the book is to enable you to investigate *why* these momentous events happened. By starting in the sixteenth century I do not want you to assume that I believe that this is where the story *must* begin. But this will allow you to judge for yourself whether seventeenth-century people like Harrington, who believed that the war had long-term origins, were right or not. In making up your own mind you have the help of a glossary (page 63), which explains difficult terms, and a biographical section (page 61). The biographies identify some of the people quoted in the book. From this information you might be able to judge whether they are likely to be biased, or writing to form a particular viewpoint. This will help you to weigh up the reliability of particular sources. Some of these sources are discussed, too, and you should read the section on sources (page 60) now, to give yourself a clear idea of the main types included, and their strengths and weaknesses.

# The Story of the Civil War, 1642-46

*The map on the left shows the battles of the Civil War (with main battles underlined), while the map on the right indicates the relative strengths of the two sides in 1643. The King's strengths were mainly in the West and North while Parliament was strong in the Eastern Counties. A triangle between Gloucester, Arundel and Lyme Regis was fiercely contested by both sides. Those living in this area and more especially in the Thames Valley experienced some of the worst fighting*

In the course of this book you will be trying to work out why Englishmen who might have served alongside one another as J.P.s or sat together in Parliament should spend nearly four years fighting one another on the battlefield. It is as well to remember that most wars – civil wars included – are started by minorities of committed people – religious zealots, politicians, men of power and wealth, kings.

It used to be thought that the English Civil War had little impact on the lives of ordinary people. There is a story told, supposedly of the time, to illustrate the fact that many people were uninvolved in and generally unaware of the clashes between King and Parliament. Just before the battle of Marston Moor, a farmer appeared ready to plough the fields on which the battle was to be fought. When it was pointed out that a battle between Royalist and Parliamentary forces was about to start and that he should forget his ploughing, he replied, "Oh, have those two fallen out again?"

*in the war. The King's position deteriorated in 1644 when the Scots joined the Parliamentary forces, and in July 1644 the Royalist defeat at Marston Moor, near York, previously a Royalist stronghold, was a great blow to the King. Despite such a setback, Prince Rupert, the Royalist military leader, was still confident of victory. However, a year later, in July 1645, the new Parliamentary Army, the New Model, cut to pieces the Royalist forces at Langport near Bridgwater. The Civil War was effectively ended.*

*Royalist defeat at Marston Moor, 2 July 1644, meant that the King lost the North. It used to be thought that crucial battles such as this were the only incidents that disturbed ordinary life in the Civil War. In fact, 30,000 Parliamentarians had besieged the Royalist garrison for three months, before the battle. This makes the story told on page 7, about a farmer not realizing that a war was on, even less likely.*

## LIFE GOES ON AS NORMAL

It is true that for many people the main concerns of the years 1642-46 were the ordinary things such as the weather, making a living or coping with poverty.

### Diary of Ralph Josselin, Puritan minister, February 1645:

This month was dry all the time like summer on 10 and 11 day; upon 12 it rained, afterwards dry, but generally very warm, ushering in the spring; our streets all overdry, ground so hard they could ever remember the like. So it continued until March 3, then it rained. Violets were commonly blown, rose bushes fully leaved, apricots fully blossomed out.

### Bath City Council Minute Book:

Throughout the four years of the Civil War the Bath Minute Book consists of entries like the following:

November 1643: Agreed that Mr. Hayward shall have stones out of the quarry in the Common for 3d a load he being at the charge of digging them and carrying them from the lanes or Common high way.

March 31, 1645: Katherine Griffyn, a decrepit old Maid servant to Mr. Richard Chapman, is admitted by generall consent unto the Almehouse of the Blue gown for life.

The only reference to the war is the following:

May 13, 1644: Agreed that a Collection be made throughout the Citie for Prince Maurice [brother of Rupert, leader of Royalist forces].

**THE IMPACT OF THE WAR**

There is in fact a good deal of evidence to suggest that the Civil War had a considerable impact on the lives of many people. The tenants of William Davenport, a gentleman who lived at Bramhall near Stockport in Cheshire, were sufficiently aware of the issues over which the war was being fought to opt for Parliament while Davenport tried to remain neutral.

### Letter to William Davenport from some of his tenants:

Much honoured Sir,
We your Worship's tenants . . . doe most humbly intreat your Worshipe that either you would be pleased to bend your intencions that way which wee may with upright harts and saffe consciencies cleave to you both in lyffe and death [i.e. they hope Davenport can support Parliament] or else that your Worship will not repute us with [i.e. accuse us of being] ill-affected or false-hearted tenants in refusinge to venture our lyves in causes that our harts and consciences maintayne and deffend you in. . . . For howsoever we would not for the world harbour a disloyal thought against his Maiestie yett we dare not lifte up our handes against the honourable assembly of Parliament whom we are conffydently assured doe labour both the happiness of his Maiestie and all his kingdom.

(*Source:* Letter Book of William Davenport)

You should note the argument of Davenport's tenants that in supporting Parliament they are not really opposing the King; in effect they are merely waiting for the King to recognize the good sense of Parliament's arguments.

**GOOD FRIENDS SEPARATED BY THE WAR**

Good friends were sometimes divided by the war. William Waller found himself leading a Parliamentary army while his friend, Sir Ralph Hopton, led the Royalist forces.

### William Waller to Sir Ralph Hopton:

Sir,
The experience which I have had of your worth, and the happinesse which I have enjoyed in your friendship, are wounding considerations to me when I look upon this present distance between us: certainly Sir, my affections to you are so unchangeable, that hostilitie itself cannot violate my friendship to your person; but I must be true to the cause wherein I serve. . . . That Great God, who is the searcher of all hearts, knows with what sad fear I go upon this service, and with what a perfect hate I detest a war without an enemie; but I look upon it as *opus Domini* which is enough to silence all passion in me. The God of Peace send us, in his good time, the blessing of peace and in the mean time fit us to receive it. We are both on the stage and must act those parts that are assigned to us in this Tragedy, but let us do it in the way of honour and without personal

animositie; whatsoever the issue of it be, I shall never resigne that dear title of

Your most,<br>
Affectionate Friend<br>
and Faithful Servant<br>
William Waller.

(*Source: The Pyltouse Papers Concerning the Civil War*)

## PASSIONS RUN HIGH

For some, passions ran high and there was no "gentlemanly" feeling between the sides. On 3 September 1643 William Waller, trying to defend Gloucester, received a message shot into the town by an arrow:

These are to let you understand that your God, Waller, hath forsaken you. . . . Essex [another Parliamentary leader] is beaten like a dog. Yield to the King's mercie in time, otherwise if we enter perforce no quarter [will be given] for such obstinate traiterly rogues.

From a Well-Wisher.

(*Source: Civil War in Hampshire*, ed. R.G.N. Goodwin, 1882)

Lady Derby, a Royalist, was totally unimpressed by requests from Colonel Rigby to hand over Latham House in Lancashire in 1643. Lady Derby wrote:

Tell that insolent rebel, he shall have neither persons nor house; when our provision is spent we shall find a fire more merciful than Rigby; and then if the providence of God prevent it not, my goods and my house shall

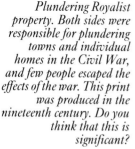

*Plundering Royalist property. Both sides were responsible for plundering towns and individual homes in the Civil War, and few people escaped the effects of the war. This print was produced in the nineteenth century. Do you think that this is significant?*

burn in his sight. My self, children and soldiers rather than fall into his hands will seal our religion and loyalty in the same flame.

(*Source: Civil War in Lancashire 1642-51*, E. Broxap, 1910, p. 108)

For many people the Civil War brought personal suffering and hardship at the hands of the respective armies. William Blundell, the Cavalier, recorded the following in his letters:

The war between King Charles and his Parliament began A.D. 1642. That year 18 March my thigh was broken with a shot in the king's service. Anno Domini 1643 all my lands and most of my goods were sequestered for being a Papist and a Delinquent.

(*Source:* Letters of William Blundell to his Friends, 1620-98)

### The Royalist attack on Cirencester:

The war was brutal, with many innocent people suffering, as a Royalist description of Prince Rupert's attack on Cirencester makes clear:

The town yielded much plunder from which the undistinguishing soldiers could not be kept, but which was equally injurious to friend and foe; so that many honest men, who were imprisoned by the rebels [i.e. Parliament] for not concurring with them, found themselves undone altogether [i.e. killed by Royalist troops].

(*Source:* Clarendon, *History of the Great Rebellion*, vol. 3, p. 417)

### Another description of the capture of Cirencester:

A few days afterwards, Prince Rupert, with 4,000 horse and foot, marched by Sudeley Castle to Cirencester where the magazine of the County lay; this he took putting the Earl of Stamford's regiment and many others to the sword; took 1,000 prisoners and 3,000 arms.

Then the prisoners were led in triumph to Oxford, where the King and Lords looked on them, and too many smiled at their misery, being tied with cords, almost naked, beaten and driven along like dogs.

(*Source: Whitelock Memorials*, 1732 ed., p. 167)

### Economic misery:

The combination of heavy taxation and free quartering of soldiers brought economic misery, as Henry Townshend describes for Worcestershire:

The County is fallen into such want and extremity [because of] the number and oppression of the Horse lying upon free quarter that the people are necessitated (their Hay being spent) to feed their horses with corn, whilst their children are ready to starve for want of Bread.

This exacting of free quarter and extorting of sums of money for the time of their absence from their quarters mingled with threats of firing their Houses, their persons with death, and their goods with pillaging. . . .

Their daily robberies of all Market people killing and wounding men who resist . . . their contempt of all discipline, disobedience to all orders. . . .

That the Insolencies, oppressions and cruelties have already so disaffected and disheartened the people that they are grown desperate and are already upon the point of rising everywhere. . .

(*Source:* Diaries of Henry Townshend, 1645)

A recent historian confirmed the picture painted by Henry Townshend:

For most inhabitants of England and Wales the Civil Wars were an experience unlike anything they had known before . . . in 1642 life changed. The next four years brought to some places utter disaster; to others little more than heavy taxation and alarming changes in sources of authority and justice. . . . Most of all there was fear – the new and inescapable fear that the soldiers would come. They could descend on a town, a village or a house. They could stay for a day or for a few weeks or for years. They could take a few household possessions or destroy the means of livelihood.

(*Source:* Donald Pennington, "The War and the People" in *Reactions to the English Civil War*, ed. John Morrill, Macmillan, 1982)

---

*THINGS TO DO AND THINK ABOUT:*

*Try to find out what happened in your own area in the Civil War. There is a list of local publications on page 61 and local libraries or records offices might help.*

*If you can do this, make out a date chart of the main events. From that you might go on to keep a diary in the style of Ralph Josselin, revealing your concern about everyday problems of seventeenth-century life, but also the particular concerns of the Civil War.*

*If you are unable to research into your local area, use the evidence of this chapter to write a letter to a friend expressing your fears or lack of them that the Civil War will affect your life. You should declare whether you are a Royalist, a Parliamentarian or neutral.*

---

# Filling in the Background:
# Social Change, 1540-1640

James Harrington, writing in the 1650s, was one of the first writers to link the English Civil War with social changes over the previous hundred years. Harrington provided a model for later historians when he argued that a change in the distribution of wealth within society inevitably resulted in a different political system. In early seventeenth-century England, he said, the decline of the aristocracy was almost bound to bring down the monarchy.

> The dissolution of the late monarchy was as natural as the death of a man. . . . Oceana, or any other nation of no greater extent must have a competent nobility, or is altogether incapable of monarchy; for where there is equality of estates there must be equality of power, and where there is equality of power there can be no monarchy. . . . A monarchy divested of her nobility hath no refuge under heaven but an army. Wherefore the dissolution of this Government caused the War, not the War the dissolution of this government.

(*Source:* James Harrington, *The Commonwealth of Oceana*, 1656)

**SOCIAL DIVISION** Before attempting to test out Harrington's theory against the available evidence, you need to look at the social structure of pre-Civil War England. Professor Lawrence Stone has divided sixteenth- and seventeenth-century English society into six groups, while emphasizing that the most fundamental division was between groups 4 to 6 on the one hand, and groups 1 to 3 on the other.

Groups 4-6 were the major landowners in the country, and also those who possessed political power. Group 6, the nobility or aristocracy, had the greatest political and economic power in 1540, but not necessarily in 1640. Group 5, the upper gentry, were the class from whom the Justices of the Peace (see page 24) were likely to be chosen. This was the group that controlled local county government. Group 4 were the dominant group in the parishes. Below group 4 few people exercised political power, though the yeomen in group 3 might be parish officials. Also, some yeomen were quite wealthy, and some were pushing themselves into group 4 in the sixteenth century. Below the yeomen in the social scale, groups 1 and 2 had neither wealth nor power and in that century their position worsened.

Group 1  The dependents on charity whether widows, aged or unemployed; also the apprentices and living-in servants, who composed as much as 15-25% of the adult population.
Group 2  The living-out labourers, both rural and urban, agricultural and industrial.
Group 3  The husbandmen and the lesser yeomen (both tenants and freeholders) and the more substantial yeomen; also the artisans, shopkeepers and small internal traders.

Group 4   The lesser or parish gentry.

Group 5   The upper gentry; squires, knights and baronets.

Group 6   The peers; barons, viscounts, earls, marquises and dukes.

(*Source:* Lawrence Stone, *The Causes of the English Revolution, 1529-1642*, Routledge and Kegan Paul, 1972)

## POPULATION GROWTH LEADS TO INFLATION

In the period 1540-1640 a number of economic changes were making an impact on English society. There was a rise in population, from about 3 million to 5 million, in England and Wales. This added enormously to the work force, increased the mobility of labour and produced larger towns. After 1620, however, evidence suggests a slowing down of the population increase in every area except the north-west of England. Plague, a shortage of land and emigration were responsible for this.

Population growth means that more people are looking for food and other goods. If supplies of such goods do not increase sufficiently, prices simply rise. Largely as a result of the population growth, there was a dramatic increase in prices of between 400% and 650% from 1500 to 1640. The price rise affected all sections of society. Real wages declined sharply so that labourers became poorer, and could often not afford bread made from wheat.

Yet such a price of corn continueth in each town and market . . . that the poor labouring man is not able to reach unto it, but is driven to content himself with horse corn, I mean beans, peas, oates, tares and lintels. . . . If the world last awhile after this rate wheat and rye will be no grain for poor men to feed on. . .

(*Source:* Simon D'Ewes, *Journal of the Parliaments of Elizabeth*, p. 162, published 1693)

This situation resulted in an increase in riots, especially when food prices were particularly high.

## INFLATION AND LANDOWNERS

While inflation brought poverty to large sectors of the population, it offered prospects for good profits to those who held and farmed land. High prices for wheat and also for wool encouraged farmers to enclose their lands to make them more productive. Moreover, perhaps as much as 30% more land was available for commercial development in the sixteenth century as a result of the Crown selling off its own lands as well as monastic and other Church lands. The Crown sold off land in this way because it was getting poorer as a result of inflation. Under such pressures, a more commercial approach to land was adopted: rents which had not risen in the 150 years before 1500 had gone up by as much as eight times on some estates by 1600. Society was becoming increasingly dominated by money, as a seventeenth-century source suggests:

To have money is to be master of every almost desirable adjustement to God's glory and men's good. Money being thus prevalent it cannot be denied to be a probable use to men and in them to families.

(*Source:* E. Waterhouse, *Gentleman's Monitor*, 1665)

There is little doubt that inflation had a very important impact on all landowners. Those who changed their methods of economic management, enclosed land and put up their rents gained from the sixteenth- and early seventeenth-century price rise. The more conservative landlords who kept to the old ways were getting poorer. It seems likely that there were more innovating landlords among the gentry than among the aristocracy, and that on balance the gentry emerged as a richer class by 1640 than they had been in 1540. But R.H. Tawney's argument that this represented a change in the class system with a "rise of the gentry" and a "decline of the aristocracy" is an exaggeration. Nevertheless, there is more evidence to support Tawney than another historian, Trevor-Roper, who argued that most gentry were suffering economic decline in this period.

## Two historians differ:

In 1941 R.H. Tawney combined Harrington's ideas of seventeenth-century change with his own analysis of the impact of inflation on groups 4 and 5. In two articles, *Harrington's Interpretation of his Age* and *The Rise of the Gentry 1558-1640*, Tawney argued that the gentry rose at the expense of the nobility.

The fate of the conservative was, in fact, an unhappy one. Reduced to living 'like a rich beggar' in perpetual want, he sees his influence, popularity and property all melt together. . . . But the conditions which depressed some incomes inflated others; and while one group of landowners bumped heavily along the bottom, another that was quicker to catch the tide when it turned, was floated to fortune.

(*Source:* R.H. Tawney, *The Rise of the Gentry*, 1941)

The hard-headed gentry "floated to fortune" while the aristocracy, lacking the commercial drive, went under. The Civil War, according to Tawney, was caused by the gentry class trying to get more political power to equal their increased wealth and status.

Not so, said Professor Trevor-Roper in 1953, who then offered his own theory of the causes of the Civil War. According to Trevor-Roper the gentry were not increasing their wealth and power; in fact, ordinary gentry who had no income other than from land (including those in Stone's group 5) were suffering a decline in their fortunes as they failed to keep their profits above inflation. The only gentry to make money were those who became favourites of the monarch and received office. He pointed to such royal servants as William Cecil and his son Robert, who after service to Elizabeth I and James I spent lavishly on Hatfield House and Burghley House. The Civil War was caused by the resentment of the disgruntled mere gentry against the King and his Court favourites.

**THE EVIDENCE**  We will now look at the kind of evidence which Tawney and Trevor-Roper used to arrive at their different conclusions.

## William Harrison:

William Harrison was a country parson with an interest in topography and chronology.

*Many new gentry houses built in the sixteenth and seventeenth centuries were similar to the Elizabethan house at Gawthorp, Yorkshire, shown here. Built of either stone or brick, with extensive use of glass, they reflected the growing prosperity of the gentry. By consulting local guide books or your tourist office you could find out how many country houses in your area were first built in the sixteenth or seventeenth century.*

The furniture of our houses also exceeds [earlier houses] and is grown in the manner even to passing delicacy. . . . Likewise in the houses of gentlemen and some other wealthy citizens it is not [unusual] to behold generally their greatest provision of tapestry, Turkey work, pewter, brass, fine linen and thereto costly cupboards of plate worth £500 or £600 or £1,000. Both herein all these sorts do exceed their elders and predecessors.

(*Source:* William Harrison, *Description of England*, published 1577)

*With the expansion of overseas trade and the growth of the cloth trade in certain areas of the country, a number of merchants became rich enough to build impressive houses. Merchant houses such as this one in King's Lynn were likely to be built of local materials. Since East Anglia has little stone, many houses like this were wooden-framed with plaster.*

A yeoman's cottage about 1600: the poor would have lived in something much less substantial. But the cottage is still fairly basic, possibly with only one room – the kitchen downstairs, with a loft as the only other room in the house. The kitchen also serves as a workplace.

## Thomas Wilson:

Thomas Wilson (c. 1560-1629) was the younger son of a gentleman, and a Government archivist.

It cannot be denied but [that] the common people are very rich albeit they be much decayed from the states they were wont to have, for the gentlemen which were wont to addict themselves to wars are now for the most part grown to become good husbands [husbandmen] and know how to improve their lands to the uttermost as the farmer and countryman, so that they take their farms into their hands as the leases expire and either till themselves or let them out to those who will give most; whereby the yeomanry of England is decayed. . .

(*Source:* Thomas Wilson, *The State of England*, 1600)

## Sir John Oglander:

Sir John Oglander (1558-1655) lived on the Isle of Wight. He was a J.P. and Deputy Governor of Portsmouth and High Sheriff of Hampshire. The following is an extract from his *Royalist Notebook*. (He fought for the King in the Civil War.)

It is impossible for a mere gentleman ever to grow rich or raise his house. He must have some other vocation with his inheritance, as to be courtier, lawyer, merchant or some other vocation. If he hath no other vocation let him get a ship and judiciously manage her or buy some auditor's place or be vice-admiral in his country. By only following the plough he may keep his word and be upright but he will never increase his fortune.

Be sure to give all thy sons a vocation and God will bless thee and them. Without this they will hardly live in this or the next world. Keep not thy children idly at home to be bird catchers or dog drivers, but be sure to settle them in a course of life – and that betimes, lest the name of gentry make them too high for it and so in the end, bring them to beggary.

---

*THINGS TO DO AND THINK ABOUT:*

*Pick out one source that supports the Tawney thesis and one that supports Trevor-Roper's argument about the causes of the Civil War. Give reasons for your choice.*

*What are the limitations of these sources in assessing the impact of the economic and social changes of the period? What other kind of sources would you like to be available?*

*Whatever the sources imply about the role of the gentry, do they suggest significant economic change in the century before the Civil War?*

---

**SUMMARY**   Such a small selection of primary sources is not sufficient to make a definite interpretation of the economic and social changes of the sixteenth and seventeenth centuries. Moreover, you probably concluded that contemporaries seem as divided as modern historians about what was happening to the gentry in this period. To add to your difficulties, the best example of a gentleman who believed that high profits could not come from land alone was Sir John Oglander. As a "disgruntled" gentleman, unable to keep pace with inflation, he might have joined Parliament, according to the Trevor-Roper thesis. Instead, he fought for the King!

There appears to be agreement among historians that the century before the Civil War was one of considerable economic and social change. The primary sources suggest bigger houses, better furniture, and above all a greater emphasis on money. There is little agreement about the fate of particular classes such as the gentry and the aristocracy within this change.

Lastly, the mere fact of social change does not mean that it was significant as a cause of the Civil War. Two very prominent historians, R.H. Tawney and H. Trevor-Roper, have argued that social factors *were* important in the Civil War, but you need not accept this. You will find other historians who reject this interpretation. You will need to examine the evidence in subsequent chapters to see whether you are convinced that men fought for or against the King for social and class reasons, or for other motives such as religion or political issues.

# Filling in the Background: Religion, 1534-1625

**RELIGION AND POLITICS**

Few historians today would deny that religion played an important part in the Civil War. Religion and politics had always been closely linked in England. Even before Henry VIII rejected the Pope and made himself Head of the Church in England in 1534, Kings had exercised a good measure of control over the Church. The clergy generally gave solid support to the King and the pulpit was often used to preach political obedience to the Crown. Moreover, bishops, in addition to governing the Church, acted as civil servants for the Crown in their particular localities. Overall, the Church provided the monarchy with its most constant support and the bishops were usually its most loyal supporters in the House of Lords. Any change in the organization of the Church, therefore, was bound to have important political repercussions.

**CATHOLICS AND PROTESTANTS**

Religion had become even more of a political issue in 1534 when Henry VIII broke with Rome, after which England ceased to be part of the Roman Catholic Church. From 1534 even to the present day England has never been united in religion; in the sixteenth and early seventeenth centuries this lack of religious unity also meant potential political conflict. In Germany, the Netherlands and France, there were "Wars of Religion" in the sixteenth century, and the great European war in the early seventeenth century, the Thirty Years War (1615-48), was caused partly by the clash between

*The Reformation in England was promoted by a good deal of propaganda, both printed and visual. In the first panel we see Henry VIII striking a blow for English independence by rejecting papal decrees, while in the second panel the new Protestant service of 1549 shows the priest and congregation together – not separated by a screen as in the Catholic service. In the third panel Mary I is depicted burning Protestants, while on the extreme right Elizabeth I receives a Bible, showing that she is bringing Protestantism back to England.*

Catholics and Protestants. In England there were no civil wars over religion. Nevertheless, there were considerable problems. Under Henry VIII the country remained basically Catholic in its beliefs, though officially separated from the Roman Catholic Church. Under Edward VI (1547-53), however, Protestantism began to spread rapidly, though many northern counties such as Lancashire resisted the new religion. Between 1553 and 1558 this pattern was completely reversed, with the accession of Mary Tudor. As a devout Catholic, she was determined to re-introduce Catholicism, and England was formally brought back into the Church of Rome. Many Protestants left England for exile, while 250 mainly lower-class people who refused to accept Catholicism were burnt as heretics.

## ELIZABETH I AND THE ANGLICAN CHURCH

Elizabeth I, therefore, inherited a difficult religious situation when she came to the throne in 1558, with every county in England containing both Protestants and Catholics. In the 1554 Religious Settlement Elizabeth restored Protestantism as the official religion, but she aimed to create a Church to which as many of her subjects as possible could subscribe. The Anglican Church, as it was known, was therefore something of a compromise. Its doctrines were very clearly Protestant, based on the beliefs of one of the great Reformation leaders, John Calvin. But the church services still contained practices, such as the wearing of vestments by the clergy and the congregation being obliged to kneel to take communion, which to more extreme Protestants were remnants of Catholicism, or "popery".

## PURITANS

On balance, the Anglican Church was a great achievement, with a majority of English people supporting it. Even most Catholics in the early part of Elizabeth's reign went to Anglican services. Only a small minority – some 1%-3% of the population – remained committed Catholics outside the Anglican Church. However, this compromise Church was attacked by the extreme Protestants, known as Puritans. They remained within the Anglican Church but they wanted to change it. Led by some clergy, but with gentry support, the Puritans wanted a Church that had eliminated all traces of "popery". Puritan clergy objected to the wearing of vestments, which they termed the "rags of the Anti-Christ". They also wanted more emphasis on preaching and less on ritual within the church service. By the 1570s a radical wing of Puritanism had emerged, consisting mainly of clergy. This group, the Presbyterians, wanted to abolish bishops within the Church and replace them with a system in which the laity would combine with the clergy to form a "presbytery" which would govern the Church and provide the discipline exercised by a bishop in the Anglican Church.

## JAMES I AND THE PURITANS

In the reign of Elizabeth, the Puritan movement, especially the non-Presbyterian kind, grew in strength. Though in the 1580s and 1590s Elizabeth did her best to suppress this growing Puritanism, it was receiving increasing protection from the gentry. The accession of James VI of Scotland as James I of England in 1603 brought renewed hope for the Puritans. James had been brought up as a Presbyterian, and so the Puritans were confident that the new King would favour the "godly" reforms advocated by them. The Puritans therefore lost no time in presenting

James with a petition for reform, as soon as he entered his new kingdom.

## The Millenary Petition 1603 presented by the Puritan Clergy to James I on his accession:

The humble petition of the ministers desiring reformation of certain ceremonies and abuses of the Church.
1. In the church service, that the cross in baptism . . . may be taken away. The cap and surplice not urged. That diverse terms of priests and absolution and some other used, with the ring in marriage, and other such like in the book may be corrected. That the Lord's day be not profaned. . . . No popish opinion to be any more taught or defended; no ministers charged to teach their people to bow at the name of Jesus.

## Hampton Court Conference, January 1604:

Following the Millenary Petition, James was quite happy to call a conference – he liked nothing better than a good debate on theology. He therefore called together representatives of the Puritans and the Anglican bishops. James listened attentively to proposals for reform from the Puritans, but he clashed with a group of Presbyterians. James's Presbyterian upbringing had not left him totally sympathetic to that form of religion. In particular, he felt that bishops were essential for good government in both Church and state. He reacted sharply, therefore, to suggestions of Presbyterianism, drawing on his experience as King of Scotland before 1603:

a Scottish Presbytery . . . agreeth as well with monarchy as God with the Devil. Then Jack and Tom and Will and Dick shall meet, and at their pleasures censure me and my Council. . . . Stay I pray you, for one seven years before you demand that of me.

Once stung by the Presbyterians, James decided to reinforce his authority over the Church by forcing the Puritans to conform to all aspects of Anglican policy.

## Proclamation enjoining conformity to the form of the service of God established, July 1604:

We have thought good once again to give notice thereof to all our subjects by public declaration . . . and consequently to admonish themselves thereunto, without listening to the troublesome spirits of some persons, who never receive contentment either in civil or ecclesiastical matters but in their own fantasies, especially of certain ministers who under pretended zeal of reformation are the chief authors of division and sect among our people. Of many of which we hope that now when they shall see that such things as they proposed for attention prove upon trial weakly grounded as deserve not admittance, they will out of their own judgement conform themselves. . .

*10 of May the Boocke of Spartes vpon the Lords day was burnt by the Hangman in the place where the Croffe ftoode, & at Exchange*

*The Puritans objected to sports being played on Sundays; the "Sabbath" had to be kept holy. When James I re-issued the Book of Sports in 1618, thus giving his support to Sunday sports, the Puritans' angry reaction included the burning of the book in London.*

The Puritans were disappointed with the outcome of the Hampton Court Conference. For some, it was the beginning of a disillusionment with the Anglican Church that led them to emigrate to America in the 1620s. But most Puritans seem to have accepted the outcome, as a recent historian has stressed:

Despite the disappointment, most [Puritan] clergy were far too committed to the ideal of a national church, to their pastoral charges, and to their livelihoods, to resist; only about ninety ministers, around 1 per cent of the total parish clergy, lost their livings.

(*Source:* Derek Hirst, *Authority and Conflict in England 1603-58*, Edward Arnold, 1986)

In addition to most Puritans accepting the Anglican Church, a number of their leaders expressed strongly monarchical views:

**William Perkins, a leading Puritan of the late sixteenth and early seventeenth century:**

God therefore hath given to kings, and to their lawful deputies, power and authority not only to command and execute his own laws, commanded in his word; but also to ordain and enact other good and profitable laws of their own, for the more particular governments of their realms. . . . . And furthermore God hath given these gods upon earth a power as to make these laws and annexe these punishments.

**Another Puritan, Robert Bolton:**

Even a contemptuous thought of a king, or lawful authority, is a sin of high nature. . .

(*Source:* quoted in K. Sharpe, *Faction and Parliament*, Clarendon Press, 1978, p. 21-24)

*Did James I have much to fear from the Puritans?*

*Does the evidence of this section suggest a serious religious clash between the King and the Puritans?*

**SUMMARY**  You need to remember that religion and politics were closely linked. Whatever James I thought of individual Puritan demands, he was determined to control the Church and not allow the Puritans, in or outside of Parliament, to dictate policy. Whether this meant a serious clash between James I and the Puritans is another matter. You might have replied to this question that two or three sources are insufficient evidence to make any judgement. You would be right to make such a conclusion. But historians also have to use negative evidence. There are, in fact, few documents from this period suggesting strong religious clashes until the 1620s. By 1621 the House of Commons, which itself was increasingly Puritan, opposed the King's pro-Spanish foreign policy. Religious and political grievances were coming together. Frustrated by James's refusal to listen to their views on foreign policy, and the King's tendency to lecture them, the House of Commons turned to stating its constitutional rights and attacking the King's leading minister.

# Filling in the Background: Politics, 1603-25

**THE MONARCH'S POWER AND ITS LIMITS**

In the sixteenth and early seventeenth centuries the monarchy was still the lynchpin of all government. The monarch was assisted in day-to-day administration by a small group of ministers known as the Privy Council. The King chose these ministers and could dismiss them at will, without reference to anyone else. It was the King, too, who called Parliament, and the monarch also had the right to dismiss it at any time, or to prorogue it.

English Kings had considerable powers. They thought themselves answerable only to God for their actions, and not to Parliament or to their subjects. In practice, however, the English King was far more limited in the power he could exercise. Though the monarch could make laws by issuing "proclamations", the highest form of law was Statute. Statute was made by the *King in Parliament*, which meant that he had to be approved by both the House of Commons and the House of Lords. Therefore the King had to call Parliament when important laws were needed.

The monarch was also dependent on Parliament for money. The King had his own sources of revenue. He received rents from Crown lands and an income from the fines levied on wrong-doers, while customs duties were an increasingly important source of revenue with the trade expansion of the sixteenth century. In addition, the Crown could raise money by selling off its lands, or, after 1534, those of the Church. For example, the sale of monastic lands from the 1540s provided a valuable addition to the royal treasury. Nevertheless, these sources were seldom sufficient for effective royal government, especially during times of war. Moreover, in the sixteenth century prices had risen five-fold; royal revenue failed to keep up with this inflation. As a result, the monarchy was becoming more dependent on Parliament to vote taxes. Since each individual grant of taxation had to be approved by Parliament, this meant it had to be called more frequently.

The King was also dependent on a wider group of gentry than those represented in Parliament, for his governing of the English counties. The key figures in local government were the Justices of the Peace, who sat at Quarter Sessions when they made judgements on both criminal and administrative matters. They reprimanded parish officials who had failed to repair roads, and punished vagrants and thieves. They also carried out instructions sent by the Privy Council.

The Justices of the Peace were unpaid. They were pleased to do the job because it gave them status, but the King could not afford to upset them too much by asking them to carry out too many policies with which they disagreed.

The Crown's reliance on unpaid J.P.s and Parliament made its power less than absolute. Moreover, Parliament was increasing its influence by the early seventeenth century. A greater number of Statutes were passed in the sixteenth century than in previous years, and this, together with its increasing financial role, meant that Parliament was taking a more active part in the government of the country. By the reign of Elizabeth I, the House of Commons, in particular, was asserting the right to speak freely on all political matters. By contrast, Queen Elizabeth believed that decisions on issues such as religion, succession and foreign policy were her prerogative and she attempted to limit discussion of these. Elizabeth was unsuccessful in preventing such discussion, but generally successful in limiting Parliament's effective influence on policy-making. When James I came to the throne in 1603, therefore, relations between the King and Parliament were delicately poised. As yet there was no confrontation between them; Parliament believed that its duty was to work *with* the King to provide good government. Nevertheless, Parliament was now prepared to assert its rights. Therefore, unless the King showed tact and skill in dealing with his Parliaments, the stage was set for a further exchange and ultimately conflict over the exact rights of Parliament against those of the monarchy. There was little tactful handling by James; instead, on a number of occasions between 1604 and 1621, he chose to lecture Parliament about its subordinate role in government.

## JAMES I AND PARLIAMENT

The House of Commons soon took the opportunity to tell the new King, James I, that Parliament, according to its own reckoning, possessed a range of rights. James, however, was not impressed by the behaviour of the Commons in asserting its rights.

**Apology of the House of Commons: 20 June 1604. To the King's most excellent Majesty, from the House of Commons:**

The rights and liberties of the Commons of England consisteth chiefly in these three things: first, that the shires, cities and boroughs of England . . . have free choice of such persons as they shall put in trust to represent them: secondly that the persons chosen during the time of the parliament, as also of their access and recess, be free from restraint arrest and imprisonment: thirdly that in parliament they may speak freely their consciences without check and controlment, doing the same with due reverence to the sovereign court of parliament, that is, to your Majesty and both the Houses, who all in this case make but one politic body, whereof your Highness is the head.

**James I's speech at the prorogation of Parliament, 7 July 1604:**

With you [My Lords] I will not be long. I will not flatter, nor by God's grace speak an untruth publicly or privately; less than this I cannot afford you, and give you your due, that you have carried yourselves with discretion, modesty, judgement, care and fidelity. Never a king had better reason to praise your subjects than I you. In fine, you have done that both in circumstance and effect that became you.

I have more to say to you, My Masters of the Lower House. . . . You see how in many things you did not well. . . . You have done many things rashly. I say not you meant disloyally. I receive better comfort in you, and account better to be king of such subjects than of so many kingdoms. Only I wish you had kept a better form. I like form as much as matter. It shows respect, and I expect it, being a king well born (suppose I say it) as any of my progenitors. I wish you would use your liberty with more modesty in time to come.

### James I's view of Kingship, 1610:

The state of monarchy is the supremest thing upon earth; for Kings are not only God's lieutenants upon earth, and sit upon God's throne, but even by God himself they are called Gods. . . . Kings are justly called Gods; for that they exercise a manner or resemblance of divine power upon earth. For, if you will consider the attributes of God, you shall see how they agree in the person of the King. God hath power to create or destroy, make or unmake, at his pleasure; to give life or send death, to judge all and not to be judged. . . . And the like power have Kings, they make and unmake their subjects: they have power of raising or casting down; of life and of death; judges over all their subjects and in all causes, and yet accountable to none but God alone.

(*Source:* speech to Parliament, 1610)

In response to James's "high" views of kingship, Parliament tries to assert that the King is under the law. The King's supreme rights, his prerogative, can be questioned by Parliament.

### Debate in committee, 22 May 1610, on Commons Petition of Right:

Mr. Fuller repeated part of a speech that was formerly spoken by Mr. Whitelock which was that the English nation was accompted in times past by all others in special respects:
1. That that which is the subjects' cannot be taken from them without their consent, but by due course of law.
2. That laws cannot be made without the consent of the three estates. That the Parliament, consisting of these three estates, was the armamentary or storehouse wherein these things were safely reposed and preserved, as well the law of the land as the rights and properties of the subjects to their lands and goods. And that the special privilege of parliament is to debate freely of all things that shall concern any of the subjects in particular, or the commonwealth in general, without any restraint or inhibition.
   . . . It was said that in all ages the king's prerogative . . . hath been examined and debated in parliament. . . . Also it was said that in all the Courts of Justice at Westminster the king's prerogative is there ordinarily disputed and therefore may much more be debated in parliament, being the highest court of justice in the realm.

---

*THINGS TO DO AND THINK ABOUT:*

*Using all the sources and the introduction to this chapter, how much do you think that James I and the House of Commons differed in their views on the* rights and role of Parliament?

*In what respects might the primary sources give a distorted view of the relationship between Crown and Parliament? Do you think that the sources are a cross-section of what went on in Parliament or might they have been selected for their dramatic qualities?*

## THE 1621 PARLIAMENT

Between 1610 and 1621 James, by various financial expedients and the avoidance of war, managed to rule without calling Parliament, except for three weeks in 1614. When Parliament met in 1621 it was initially conciliatory. It granted James £140,000 in case England should need to intervene to help the Protestants in Europe, against Spain and the Holy Roman Empire in the Thirty Years War. The House of Commons was somewhat taken aback, however, when James argued that £1 million might be needed for war. Many M.P.s believed that by combining with the Dutch and using a sea rather than a land war, the objective could be achieved more quickly and more cheaply. In fact, for James, preparations for war were only a back-up to his preferred policy of diplomacy; he hoped to persuade Spain to withdraw from the Thirty Years War as part of the marriage deal between Charles I and the Spanish Infanta. Parliament was totally opposed to this diplomatic approach and retaliated by calling for an all-out war against Spain. James threatened to arrest those M.P.s who were most openly critical of his policy and he reminded the Commons that their privileges were dependent on the mere grace of the King. This set the scene for a greater clash than had occurred hitherto. The Commons asserted its rights even more forcefully than before.

*James I had hoped to cement his friendship with Spain by arranging a marriage between Prince Charles and the Spanish Infanta, daughter of the late Philip III of Spain. But Charles and Buckingham returned to England from Spain in October 1623 announcing that the marriage was off. Here we see the celebrations – bells were rung and bonfires were lit in London – as the Puritans in particular celebrated the ending of friendship with Catholic Spain.*

**The Protestation of the Commons, 1621:**

The Commons now assembled in Parliament . . . do make this Protestation following: That the Liberties, Franchises and Privileges, and Jurisdiction of Parliament are the ancient and undoubted Birthright and Inheritance of the subjects of England; and that the arduous and urgent affairs concerning the King, State and Defence of the Realm and of the Church of England, and the maintenance and making of Laws, and the redress of mischiefs and grievances which daily happen within this Realm, are proper subjects and matter of Counsel and Debate in Parliament . . . [and] every Member of the House of Parliament hath, and of right ought to have, freedom of speech to propound, treat, reason and bring to conclusion, the same . . .

(*Source:* J. Rushworth, *Historical Collections, 1659*, Vol. 1)

### The impeachment of Sir Francis Bacon, Lord Chancellor, 1621:

Parliament then removed the King's minister, Francis Bacon, by accusing him of bribery. Since all officials took gifts, it was not difficult to make the accusation stick. The significance of the "impeachment" of Bacon lay less in the accusations of bribery than in Parliament's ability to remove a minister of the King.

The House of Commons addressed the House of Lords which carried out the impeachment or trial of Bacon:

The knights, citizens and burgesses of the Commons House of Parliament have made complaint unto your Lordships of many exhorbitant offences of bribery and corruption committed by the Lord Chancellor. We understand that your Lordships [i.e. the members of the House of Lords] are ready to give judgement on the same, wherefore I, their Speaker, in their name, do humbly demand and pray judgement against him, the Lord Chancellor, as the nature of his offence and demerits do require.

[The judgement was] 1. That the Lord Viscount St. Alban, Lord Chancellor of England, shall undergo fine and ransom of £40,000.

2. That he shall be imprisoned in the Tower during the King's pleasure.

3. That he shall for ever be incapable of any office or employment in the state or commonwealth.

4. That he shall never sit in Parliament or come within the verge of the court.

(*Source: Commons Journal I*, p. 554-63)

---

*THINGS TO DO AND THINK ABOUT:*

*Compare the 1621 Protestation with the 1604 Apology. Is the 1621 Protestation going further in asserting Parliament's rights? Look particularly at lines 2-4 of the Protestation in this respect.*

*Why could the legal process of impeachment also be seen as a political weapon used by Parliament against the King?*

---

**SUMMARY** There are no easy answers to the questions you have been looking at arising out of the sources. The documents suggest a considerable difference between King and Parliament, but it may be that such clashes were newsworthy, while unspectacular examples of the King and Parliament working well together received little contemporary comment. Moreover, it is difficult to pick out a particular date or even one event which marked a significant point in the worsening relations of Crown and Parliament. However, certain traits are emerging. Firstly, it is the House of Commons that is more prominent in asserting its rights, as in the Apology and the Protestation. It is also the Commons that starts proceedings against Bacon, although the Lords try him. Secondly, by 1621 more precise demands are made by the Commons, to discuss "affairs concerning the King, State and Defence of the Realm and of the Church of England" – i.e. all aspects of governmental policy. Thirdly, the weapon of impeachment, used against Lord Bacon, and by which Parliament showed that it could rid the country of an unpopular royal minister, was to be used again on several occasions. Despite all these developments, parliamentary power was still strictly limited.

# The Rule of Charles I from 1625-40

For Clarendon, the origins of the Civil War were to be found only in 1625, with the accession of Charles I. You have already seen significant political and religious tensions developing against a background of social change which affected the power structure within the state. But even those writers, both seventeenth- and twentieth-century, who stress the importance of long-term factors, would not argue that civil war was *inevitable* in 1625. The decisive events leading to that calamity took place between 1625 and 1642.

There are certain important events and connected with them key questions that you need to ask of this period. Firstly, why did Charles I, having called three Parliaments between his accession in 1625 and 1629, decide in 1629 that he was going to govern for some time without calling Parliament? Secondly, and crucially, was Charles I making a success of ruling without Parliament up until 1637? Some of his policies were undoubtedly unpopular, but was there sufficient opposition to challenge the King before the crisis of 1637, provoked by Laud's attempts to impose the Anglican Prayer Book on the Scots? If you decide that Charles I was succeeding up to 1637, then obviously the "Bishops' War" resulting from the clash with the Scots becomes the most important single factor which led to Charles recalling Parliament in 1640. Thirdly, you will need to work out why Charles I and Parliament failed to reach an acceptable compromise between 1640 and 1642 – but that will be dealt with on pages 43-53.

**1625-29**    Charles's reign started in unfortunate circumstances. The Plague broke out in 1625 and before the end of the year 20% of London's population was dead. Protestants were convinced that this was a sign of God's disapproval of Charles's policy of granting limited toleration to Catholics. The new King also inherited an empty treasury, and since Charles was planning a war against Spain, he needed to call Parliament. Parliament approved of the war against Spain but soon quarrelled with the King over three issues – money, religion and the conduct of Charles's favourite courtier and leading minister, the Duke of Buckingham.

**MONEY**    Once Parliament assembled in 1625, conflict over money began immediately. Parliament granted the King tonnage and poundage, a form of customs duty, for one year only, instead of the customary grant for the whole reign. Why Parliament did this is not totally clear, but it was probably linked to their growing dislike and distrust of the Duke of Buckingham. Buckingham was Lord Admiral, and since tonnage and poundage was revenue granted for the protection of the seas, its limitation seemed an appropriate weapon against the Duke. The 1625 Parliament however did grant the King money for the war against Spain. But the English attack on Cadiz in September 1625 was a total failure. Consequently, the 1626 Parliament was reluctant to grant any further taxes. Charles impatiently dismissed Parliament and instead decided to raise money by levying a forced loan.

## The forced loan:

Clarendon argues that Parliament would have granted the King the money asked for (five subsidies), but this seems unlikely.

In the second Parliament [1626] there was a mention, and intention, and intention declared, of granting five subsidies, a proportion . . . never before heard of in Parliament. And that meeting [i.e. Parliament] being, upon very unpopular and unplausible reasons, immediately dissolved, those five subsidies were exacted throughout the whole kingdom with the same rigour as if, in truth, an Act had passed to that purpose. And very many gentlemen of prime quality, in all the several counties of England, were, for refusing to pay the same, committed to prison, with great rigour and extraordinary circumstances. And could it be imagined that these men would meet again in a free convention of Parliament without a sharp and severe expostulation and inquisition into their rights and the power that had imposed on that right?

(*Source:* Clarendon, *The History of the Great Rebellion*)

The continuation of the war against Spain, which by 1627 had been extended to include hostilities against France, meant that another forced loan was levied. In addition, troops were billeted on individual communities, especially in the South of England. Any tax-payer refusing to contribute to the forced loan was imprisoned. When Charles's third Parliament met in 1628, it immediately presented the King with the Petition of Right, protesting against royal actions, especially in 1627. Charles I was forced to accept this.

## Petition of Right, 1628:

and by the authority of the Parliament, it is decreed and enacted that no person shall be compelled to make any loans to the King against his will. . . . Yet nevertheless of late . . . your people have been in diverse places assembled, and required to lend money unto your Majesty, and [some] of them, upon their refusal to do so . . . have been constrained to become bound to make appearance and give attendance before your privy council.

And whereas by the Statute called the Great Charter of Liberties of England, it is declared and enacted, that no freeman may be taken or imprisoned . . . but by lawful judgement of his peers. . . . Nevertheless divers of your subjects have of late been imprisoned without any cause showed.

And whereas of late great companies of soldiers and mariners have been dispersed into diverse counties of the realm; and the inhabitants against their wills, have been compelled to receive them into their houses, and there to suffer them to sojourn against the laws and customs of this realm, and to the great grievance and vexation of the people. . .

They do humbly pray your most excellent Majesty that no man hereafter be compelled to make any gift, or loan, benevolence, tax or such like charge, without common consent by act of parliament. . . . And that no freeman, in any such manner as is before mentioned, be imprisoned or detained. And that your majesty would be pleased to remove the said soldiers and mariners, and that your people may not be so burdened in time to come.

## THE DUKE OF BUCKINGHAM

As you have seen, dislike of the Duke of Buckingham was already influencing Parliament's attitude to the King by 1625. Parliament was frustrated by Buckingham's complete domination of the Court; it was difficult for anyone other than the supporters of Buckingham to gain access to the King. Buckingham's unpopularity increased between 1625 and 1628 as his foreign policy went from one failure to another, culminating in England's humiliating failure to help the Protestants of the Ile de Rhé off La Rochelle.

By 1628 many M.P.s saw Buckingham as the main cause of the country's problems and of the growing tensions between themselves and the King. In August of that year he was assassinated.

*A courtier, of both James I and Charles I, and a great lover of the arts, the Earl of Arundel is shown here in an appropriate "classical" setting. Arundel was once a friend of Buckingham, but they became enemies after Buckingham's rejection of the Spanish marriage (see the picture on page 27). Arundel contributed to the attacks in Parliament on Buckingham from 1626-28.*

**Parliament attacks Buckingham in 1628, but also reveals fears for its future:**

So the next day, being Wednesday, we had a message from his Majesty by the Speaker that the Session should end on Wednesday. . . . The House was much affected to be so restrained. . . . Then Sir Robert Philips spake and mingled his words with weeping. Mr. Prynne did the like, and Sir Edward Coke, overcome with passion, seeing the desolation likely to ensue, was forced to sit down when he began to speak through the abundance of tears. . . . Then Sir Edward Coke told them . . . he not knowing whether he should speak in this House again, would now do it

*This is the note written by John Felton, Buckingham's assassin, justifying the murder of the Duke. The unpopularity of the Duke of Buckingham by 1628 can be gauged from the widespread rejoicing that greeted the news of his assassination. This served to worsen relations between Charles I and his subjects as the King was genuinely grieved by the death of his favourite.*

freely, and those protested that the author and cause of all those miseries was the Duke of Buckingham, which was answered with a cheerful acclamation in the House . . . and [they voted on the] question whether they should name him in their intended Remonstrance the Sole and Principal cause of all their Miseries at home and abroad. . .

(*Source:* J. Rushworth, *Historical Collections, 1659*, Vol. 1, p. 609)

## RELIGION

1625 proved to be a turning point in religion. As you have already seen (page 20), the Church of England had followed the Protestant doctrines of Calvin ever since 1558. The Church services were still considered too "popish" by the Puritans, but by the early seventeenth century Puritan influence in the Anglican Church was growing. Despite the disappointment of the Hampton Court Conference, many Puritans remained optimistic, especially after 1611, when Abbott, a Puritan sympathizer, was made Archbishop of Canterbury.

Any such optimism was rudely shattered on Charles I's accession, when the King gave his support to a new development within the Anglican Church. This new movement was known as Arminianism. It took its name from a Dutch theologian, Arminius, who in 1610 had challenged the doctrines of Calvin in the Dutch Church, especially the central belief of predestination. In England this anti-Calvinist movement was taken up by William Laud, an Oxford-trained cleric, who by 1633 had become Archbishop of Canterbury. Laud had the full backing of Charles I.

Not only did Laud deny Calvinist doctrines; he also wanted an Anglican Church that put emphasis on ritual, including the wearing of vestments and Church music. Laud tried to limit the amount of preaching within the Church, which the Puritans considered the most important element of the service. For the Arminians, the Church service revolved around the

Communion, and to emphasize this, Laud had the Communion tables railed off and moved back to the East end of the church – the traditional and Catholic placing of the altar. From 1625, confrontation between the Arminians, supported by the King, and the Puritans, was inevitable.

The conflict over Arminianism began in 1625 when Dr Montagu, later made the King's Chaplain, wrote a book, *A New Gag for an Old Goose*, which supported Arminianism. Archbishop Abbot, a fairly Puritan bishop, addressed Montagu from the House of Lords:

> Mr. Montagu, you see what disturbance is grown in the Church and the Parliament House by the book by you lately put forth. Be occasion of no scandal or offence; and therefore this is my advice to you. Go home, review your own book. It may be diverse things have slipped you which upon better advice you will reform.

But Arminianism continued to prosper at Court, as a draft declaration by a parliamentary sub-committee complains in 1629:

> Protestants abroad are dangerously threatened. In England, popery has grown extraordinarily and is openly – sometimes even insolently – practised. There has been a subtle and pernicious growth in Arminianism which, if unchecked, will consume true religion by dividing Englishmen at home and separating them from Reformed Churches abroad. These things are due to the suspension or neglect of the laws against papists and the defence of popish doctrines by Arminian divines and the introduction of many new and offensive ceremonies.

(*Source:* quoted in Kevin Sharpe, *Faction and Parliament*, Clarendon Press, 1978)

**PARLIAMENT DISSOLVED**

The King had been vigorously attacked by Parliament for supporting Arminianism, for his financial policies and over his choice of ministers. Charles, therefore, decided that he would rule without Parliament. On 10 March 1629, an abrupt dissolution followed "the most gloomy, sad and miserable day for England that happened in the five hundred years last past". (*Source:* Commons Debates, 1629)

**THE PERSONAL RULE, 1629-40**

The main problem facing Charles I in these years was how to raise sufficient money for effective government, without calling Parliament and without creating too much opposition in the country. The Crown had no standing army, nor did it have a large number of civil servants to execute its orders. In the counties, the King had to rely on the local gentry, acting as Justices of the Peace, Sheriffs and other officials – all unpaid – to carry out his policies.

He raised money in a variety of ways. He continued to collect tonnage and poundage, though this had been forbidden by Parliament before 1629. He revived the law requiring owners of an estate worth £40 or more to receive knighthood, which entailed heavy expenses, or else avoid receiving it by a single payment to the King. Charles I also exploited his traditional "feudal dues", such as wardship, more fully. In 1634 and subsequent years, large sums were raised by the revival of the Forest Laws. An attempt was made to reassert the King's ancient rights over all forests, and those encroaching on them were fined. The Earl of Salisbury was fined £20,000 for alleged encroachment. The most famous of all Charles's financial devices was Ship Money. This was normally levied only on coastal counties, but after 1635 it was extended to inland counties and threatened to become a permanent tax.

*The controversial tax of ship money proved to be financially very successful for Charles I. However, there was always some resistance to it, though only in 1639-40 did this reach serious dimensions. We see here that as early as 1635 a number of parishioners from Great Kimble, Buckinghamshire, refused to pay the tax. Prominent among them is John Hampden Esquire who in 1637 took the King to court over the legality of ship money. You might be interested to read the original document on the right: difficult handwriting is one of the problems historians face.*

Charles I still had to make such measures effective. Throughout the 1630s he tried to increase royal control in the counties. In 1631, for example, he issued the Book of Orders. This gave more detailed instructions to J.P.s on how the Poor Law should be administered, but many county officials saw it as an attempt by the King to tighten royal control over local government in general. More significantly, Charles attempted to increase his influence over the local militias by making more use of the Lord Lieutenants, who were much more agents of the Crown than the other local officials.

**Court of Wards:**

The Master of the Court of Wards . . . had raised the revenue of that Court to the King to be much greater than it had ever been . . . by which husbandry [i.e. effort] all the rich families of England, of noblemen and gentlemen, were exceedingly incensed, looking upon what the law had intended for their protection and preservation to be now applied to their destruction. . .

(*Source:* Clarendon, *The History of the Great Rebellion*, Vol. 1, p. 198-9)

**Ship Money, 1636:**

The Lord-Keeper February 14 in the Star Chamber spake to the Judges before they went their circuits to this effect. . . . He said this was the third year his Majesty had issued Writs, requiring aid of his subjects for the guard of the dominion of the Seas and safety of the Kingdom. In the first, when they were directed to the ports and maritime places only, there was little opposition; but when in the second year they went generally throughout the Kingdom, they were disobeyed by some, in maritime as well as inland counties, and actions have been brought against persons imployed about the execution of those writs. He said none could expect the *Arcana Regis* (Secrets of the King) should be made publick, but such reasons as are fit to be opened are these:
1. Our safety is concerned, for if we lose the dominion of the seas, we lie open to all dangers.
2. We are concerned in point of honour that we keep that dominion.
3. In point of profit to preserve our trade, which inriches inland as well as maritime places, by the vent of our wool, lead and other commodities.

(*Source:* J. Rushworth, *Historical Collections, 1659*, Vol. 2, p. 262-3)

**The Hampden case:**

John Hampden, a Buckingham country gentleman, challenged the legality of Ship Money by going to court. He lost the case, but by the narrowest of margins – five out of twelve judges voted in his favour. One of Hampden's lawyers spoke:

My Lords, the Parliament . . . is best qualified to make supply [i.e. grant taxes]. His Majesty having declared the danger, they best knowing the estates of all men within the realm, are fittest, by comparing the danger and men's estates together, to proportion the aid accordingly. . .

Sir Robert Berkeley, Justice of the King's Bench:

Where Mr. Holborne [one of Hampden's lawyers] supposed a fundamental policy in the creation of the frame of this kingdom, that in case the monarch of England should be inclined to exact from his subjects at his pleasure, he should be restrained, for that he could have nothing from them but upon common consent in Parliament.

He is utterly mistaken herein. I agree Parliament to be a most ancient and supreme court where the King and Peers, as judges, are in person, and whole body of the Commons representatively [i.e. where King, Peers and Commons actually meet and act as judges]. There Peers and Commons may in a fitting way *Parler leur ment* [speak their mind] and show the estate of every part of the kingdom. . .

But the former fancied policy I utterly deny. The law knows no such king-yoking policy. . .

There are two maxims of the law of England which plainly disprove Mr. Holborne's supposed policy. The first is "that the King is a person trusted with the state of the commonwealth." The second of these maxims is "That the King cannot do wrong."

---

*THINGS TO DO AND THINK ABOUT:*

*What principle is at stake in the Hampden case?*

*Imagine you are a country gentleman faced with a demand for Ship Money after the Hampden case. How would you react? Consider all aspects of your position, including the possible consequences of refusing to pay.*

---

## ARCHBISHOP LAUD AND THE PERSONAL RULE

From the beginning of Charles's reign, William Laud was influential in the Church of England; by 1628 he was Bishop of London and in 1633 he became Archbishop of Canterbury. As well as wanting to make changes in

*William Laud, Archbishop of Canterbury. Laud was the leading exponent of a new form of Anglicanism, Arminianism, which was promoted in England after 1625. By 1633 Laud was Archbishop of Canterbury and a member of the Privy Council. As such he was a crucial individual in the Personal Rule.*

Church services, as described on page 33, Laudianism also had an important political side. It stood for the restoration of authority. There was a stress on hierarchy and the power of the clergy. In a practical sense, Laud attempted to restore the wealth and status of the Church. He tried to win back "appropriated tithes" – income which had found its way into gentry hands instead of supporting the clergy. He was prepared to use the Church courts, especially the High Commission, to press clerical claims. Many local gentry, not just Puritan gentlemen, were hostile to this attempted revival.

### Archbishop Laud's innovations:

This year [1634] being the first of Bishop Laud's translation to Canterbury, great offence was taken at his setting up pictures in the windows of his Chappels at Lambeth and Croydon, the portraiture being made according to the Roman Missal, his bowing towards the Table or Altar, and using Copes [a vestment] at the Sacrament which people clamoured against as popish, superstitious and idolatrous. . .

Mr. Chancery, Minister of Ware in Hertfordshire, for the opposing the making of a rail about the Communion Table in that Parish Church was brought into the High Commission and suspended from the ministry.

(*Source:* J. Rushworth, *Historical Collections, 1659*, Vol. 2)

### Clarendon: the High Commission:

Persons of honour and great quality, of the court and of the country were every day cited into the High Commission court . . . and as the shame was never forgotten, but watched for revenge, so the fines imposed were the more questioned and repined against because they were assigned to the rebuilding and repairing of St. Paul's Church. . . . and [this] sharpened many man's humours against the bishops before they had any ill intention towards the Church.

(*Source: History of the Great Rebellion*, Vol. 1, p. 125)

### Laud's style:

Laud was resented for his grandiose style of living:

But see the prelate of Canterbury, in his ordinary garb, riding from Croydon to Bagshot with forty or fifty gentlemen, well mounted, attending upon him; two or three coaches, with four and six horses apiece in them, all empty, waiting upon him; two or three dainty steeds of pleasure, most rich in trappings and furniture, likewise led by him; and whenever he comes, his gentlemen ushers and his servants crying out "Room, room for my lord's grace is coming." And all this is true, if *vox populi* and fame may be credited, which is a good plea in their court. Now what I pray, could be done more to the King's Majesty or Queen, or the Prince of Wales or to the royal blood?

(*Source: The Letany of John Bastwick, 1637* p. 5-6)

*hn Bastwick, a vehement uritan, friend of William Prynne, and a writer of pamphlets against Archbishop Laud and rminianism. Like Prynne he suffered the brutal nishment of ear-cropping at the hands of Laud.*

**A trial in Star Chamber:**

One of Laud's celebrated disputes was with three leading Puritans, Prynne (a barrister), Burton (a minister) and Bastwick (a physician). They were tried in Star Chamber.

Mr Prynne . . . said if he but knew into what times they were cast, and what changes of law, religion and ceremonies had been made of late by one man [Archbishop Laud] they would look about them. They might see that no degree or profession was exempted from the prelate's malice; here is a divine for the soul, a physician for the body, and a lawyer for the estates, and the next to be censured in Star Chamber is likely to be a bishop. . . . The Archbishop of Canterbury, being informed by his spies what Mr. Prynne said, moved the Lords sitting in the Star Chamber that he might be gagged . . . [The three were finally sentenced.] Mr. Burton . . . the executioner cut off his ears deep and close, in a cruel manner, with much effusion of blood, an artery being cut, as there was likewise of Dr. Bastwick. Then Mr. Prynne's cheeks were seared with an iron made exceedingly hot; which done the executioner cut off one of his ears and a piece of his cheek with it; then hacking the other ear almost off, he left it hanging and went down; but being called up again he cut it quite off.

(*Source:* J. Rushworth, *Historical Collections, 1659*, vol. 2, p. 293-4)

---

*THINGS TO DO AND THINK ABOUT:*

*Is there any reason to suspect the objectivity of the source "The Letany of John Bastwick"?*

*How do you think English gentlemen and the professions viewed their treatment in Star Chamber?*

---

Laud's religious policy and Charles's financial measures would suggest a strong degree of unpopularity for the government by 1637. But the historian is still faced with problems. How widespread was the opposition to royal government? There was no Parliament through which grievances could be *lawfully* expressed. Did people feel strongly enough to defy the government openly and even illegally? There is little evidence of this; in fact, 1637 seems to have been a relatively calm year.

In October 1637 John Burghe wrote to the English ambassador in Paris:

All things are at this instant here in that calmness that there is very little matter of novelty to write, for there appears to be no change or alteration either in court or affairs, for all business goes undisturbedly on in the strong current of the present time to which all men for the most part submit, and that effects this quietness. And although payments here are great (considering the people heretofore have not been accustomed to them) yet they only privately breathe out a little discontented humour and lay down their purses, for I think the great tax of ship money is so well digested (the honour of the business sinking now into apprehension and among most winning an affection to it) I suppose will become perpetual...

(*Source:* quoted in Sharpe, "Personal Rule of Charles I", *Before the Civil War*, ed. Tomlinson, Macmillan, 1981)

**THE SCOTTISH CRISIS**

From the start of his reign Charles's actions towards Scotland seemed calculated to offend the Scots. In 1625 Charles declared, on the flimsiest of legal grounds, that all grants of Church and Crown land made in Scotland since 1540 were to be revoked. Scottish visitors to the English court were looked down upon there as uncultured boors. But it was Charles's religious policy that most offended Scotland.

The Lowlands of Scotland in particular were strongly Presbyterian. However, as early as 1633, when the King visited Scotland, he indicated that he meant to promote Arminianism in his Northern Kingdom as well as in England. In 1637 Charles imposed a new Prayer Book in Scotland which laid down Church services on Arminian lines. Moreover, the Prayer Book was imposed without reference to Parliament or to the General Assembly of the Church. This move caused an outrage, with rioting in Edinburgh. Even the Earl of Montrose, not an extremist, saw the new Prayer Book as the "brood of the bowels of the whore of Babylon".

## The new Prayer Book in Edinburgh:

Accordingly it [the New Prayer Book] was then begun to be read in Edinburgh in St. Giles's Church . . . many of the Council, both Archbishops, divers other Bishops, the Lords of the Session, the Magistrates of Edinburgh and a great auditory being present. No sooner had the Dean of Edinburgh opened the Book, but there were among the meaner sort (especially the women) clapping of hands and hideous execrations and outcries. The Bishop of Edinburgh (who was to preach) went into the pulpit, thinking to appease the tumult, and presently a stool was thrown at his head . . . there were outcries, rapping at the doors, and throwing in stones at the windows, crying "A Pope, a Pope, Antichrist, pull him down", that the Bailiffs were forced to come again to appease their fury. Service and sermon ended, the Bishop of Edinburgh repairing home, was near trodden to death but rescued by some who observed his danger. . .

*The people of Edinburgh meeting to sign the Covenant which refused to accept the new Laudian Prayer Book for the Church in Scotland. They claimed that this was a Covenant with God and this heightened the Scottish Protestant sense of being God's chosen nation.*

(*Source:* J. Rushworth, *Historical Collections, 1659*, Vol. 2, p. 298-9)

By February 1638 a third of the clergy and more of the nobility had signed a covenant to defend the Scottish Church. The Scottish "Covenanters" were prepared to take up arms against Charles I. By June 1639 the King

was forced to make concessions to the Covenanters in the Treaty of Berwick, but he had no intention of capitulating to the Scots. He therefore decided to call Parliament in April 1640, in order to raise money for an attack on the Scottish rebels.

The Scottish Crisis was significant for a number of reasons. Firstly, it showed that, despite the success of the government in raising money in the 1630s, the King could not cope financially with a war without calling Parliament. Secondly, the calling of Parliament gave the nation its first opportunity for a decade to express its grievances. Thirdly, the crisis heightened the religious tensions in England. The Puritans sympathized with the Scottish Covenanters and their armed challenge gave encouragement to Charles's opponents in England. Moreover, the King took certain measures which were positively provocative on the religious front. Increasingly, in the 1630s, Charles's court had gained a reputation for favouring Catholics and Catholic sympathizers. In 1639 the King appointed a Catholic sympathizer, the Earl of Arundel, as Commander of the royal forces. Soon after his appointment Arundel rode conspicuously through London with Con, the papal ambassador. For those Puritans who believed in an international papal conspiracy, this seemed to confirm their worst fears.

**THE "SHORT PARLIAMENT"**

The Parliament that Charles called in April 1640 produced such widespread criticism of royal policies that it survived a mere three weeks – hence its title, the "Short Parliament". Encouraged by his toughest minister, the Earl of Strafford, the King decided to prepare for a second war against the Scottish Covenanters, despite the absence of any parliamentary finance. Although Charles resorted to the use of desperate financial expedients, such as seizing bullion from merchants, there was insufficient money for the war and the troops were of poor quality. In August 1640 the King's forces were comprehensively defeated by the Scots at Newburn on Tyne; the Scots were in control of Northumberland and held the City of Newcastle. The King had now no option but to recall Parliament, which he did in November 1640.

---

*THINGS TO DO AND THINK ABOUT:*

*Modern historians disagree about the likely fate of Charles's Personal Rule. Professor Rubb has recently written: "The attempt to do without parliament in the 1630s was in the long run untenable. . . . Resistance to Charles's policy was inevitable."*

*Kevin Sharpe has replied: "But was it? To those on the road during the 1630s the journey seemed far from a headlong rush towards conflict. Even looking backwards from a knowledge of later events, Edward Hyde, no uncritical flatterer of Charles I, recalled the Personal Rule as a decade of calm and felicity."*

*Putting together all your previous exercises, finally debate these judgements.*

---

# The Long Parliament and the Coming of the War, 1640-42

There could be no civil war before 1642 because there was no royalist party. The origins of the English Civil War were really concerned less with the rise of opposition than with the re-surgence of loyalism; loyalty to a King who appeared to have disregarded the rights of his subjects. . .

(*Source:* J. Morrill, *The Revolt of the Provinces*, Longman, 1980, p. 13)

Charles I was forced to call the "Long Parliament" in November 1640 because the country was in crisis. The "Short Parliament" earlier in the year had lasted only three weeks, but with the Scots invading the North of England and the King with insufficient money to raise an adequate force to meet them, a new Parliament had to be called. Within two years of its calling, there was civil war in England. There are three central questions to which you need to direct your attention. Firstly, which were the major grievances that were felt by the country and Parliament between 1640 and 1642? Secondly, why were these issues of conflict between the King and Parliament not settled? And thirdly, how did the King gain a party by 1642 when there was such united opposition to him in 1640?

There are two kinds of evidence which you can use to investigate what were the major themes in 1640-41. Many petitions were sent from the counties to Westminster in this period, reflecting people's grievances and hopes. Also the Long Parliament immediately embarked on certain reforms which showed its priorities.

**PETITIONS**

Before you look at the petitions, you need to understand what was happening in the country in 1640. The winter of 1639-40 had been bleak, with a deepening economic depression, particularly in cloth-making areas. This, and agitation against enclosures, led to extensive rioting. Moreover, as you have seen, the Scottish Covenanters were threatening England. Politically, the most significant aspect of the "Scottish crisis" was the reluctance of many Englishmen to oppose the Covenanters. The Earl of Northumberland protested that many of the army collected in 1640 to fight the Scots were "readier" to draw their swords upon their own officers. Indeed, the King's troops seemed much keener to show their Puritan sympathies than to fight the Scots. Two Catholic officers were lynched and numerous altar rails broken or burnt as the troops marched north. On a wider political front the effect of the Scottish crisis was a forging of closer links between the English Puritans and the Scots. By the late 1630s there is evidence for the first time of a strong Presbyterian element in English Puritanism; by 1640 the call for the abolition of bishops was widespread.

## Herefordshire Grand Jury Presentment [Petition], 12 January 1641:

Item wee doe also finde and present that the late taxacon [taxation] upon this County for raiseinge of Money for buildings and Maintenance of shipps of warre for these five yeares last past hath bynne a great chardge greevance and Impoverishings to the Comon wealth of same; from which the said County desire to be freed; And alsoe doe finde and present that the levyinge of the unlawfull taxe of coate and Conduct money within this County hath likewyse bynne a great chardge and trouble to the whole County...

We alsoe finde and present that the iron Mills in generall within this County have bynne a generall distracon [destruction] of Trees Tymber and Coppice wood some of which being within five miles of the Cittie of Hereford, in soe much that the said Cittie is already in great want and scarcity of wood ... that if it should Contynue it would tend to the greate impoverishinge of the Inhabitants of the said Citty and many places adjacent to the same.

### From The Humble Petition of the Freeholders and the reste of the inhabitants within the county of Chester:

Therefore we humbly Petition you this honourable Assembly that you couragiously proceed against these his [i.e. the King's] mightie enemies and secret underminers of the good estate of our Church and Commonwealth and utterly dissolve their offices, which give life to the most superstitious practices in or about the worship of God: And so together with the ruine of their Antichristian Offices and Government, their corrupt Canons, booke of Articles, the English refined Masse-book of Common Prayer, with all their popish significant Ceremonies therein contained; the strict imposing whereof hath driven out of this our English nation many of our most godly and able Ministers and other his Majesties loyall subjects, able both for person and estate to have done good service to God, our King and Countrie.

### The Humble Petition of many of his Majesty's subjects in and about the City of London:

That whereas the government of archbishops and lord bishops, deans and archdeacons etc. with their courts and ministrations in them, have proved prejudicial and very dangerous both to the Church and the Commonwealth ... and occasion of many evils, pressures and grievances of a very high nature unto His Majesty's subjects in their own consciences, liberties and estates, as in a schedule of particulars hereunto annexed may in part appear...

We humbly, most humbly pray and beseech this honourable assembly that the said government, with all its dependencies, roots and branches, may be abolished and all laws in their behalf made void ... and we your humble suppliants, as in duty we are bound, will daily pray for His Majesty's long and happy reign over us.

---

*THINGS TO DO AND THINK ABOUT:*

*From the three petitions, which issues do you think are most strongly felt by the petitioners?*

*How representative do you think those three petitions were of the country as a whole?*

You probably reacted to the questions by pointing out the weakness of relying on three petitions alone to judge the mood of the whole country. It is interesting, however, that Chester in the north-west of England, not noted for its Puritanism, should be saying similar things to the radical City of London. Nevertheless, we need to know much more about how such petitions were collected before we can conclude that they were representative even of the whole county or city. A number of counties sent in more than one petition to the Long Parliament between 1640-42, and they were sometimes markedly different, especially on religious issues. In fact, initially, we cannot say any more of one petition than that it represents the views of a dominant local group or faction and their supporters. If, however, you read a sufficiently wide range of petitions, then you should see the issues that dominated the debate in 1640-42.

**REFORMS OF THE LONG PARLIAMENT**

The main aim of the Long Parliament was to tackle the grievances raised by the Personal Rule of Charles I. In general, Parliament wanted to ensure that the system of government of the 1630s was dismantled and would not occur again. The leading ministers of the King were attacked. The Earl of Strafford was impeached and sent to the Tower on 11 November 1640, and so was Archbishop Laud on 19 December. Major opponents of Laud, such as William Prynne, were released with compensation.

## The Triennial Act, February 1641:

One of the first major acts passed by Parliament was meant to make sure that the King could never rule without Parliament again. Consequently, the act laid down that Parliament had to meet once in three years, and to sit for a minimum of fifty days.

Be it enacted . . . that in case there be not a parliament summoned by writ under the Great Seal of England and assembled and held before the tenth day of September which shall be in the third year next after the last day of the last meeting and sitting in this present parliament . . . the parliament shall assemble and be held in the usual place at Westminster in such manner and by such means only as is hereafter in this present Act declared. . . .
. . . And it is further enacted that no parliament henceforth to be assembled shall be dissolved or prorogued within fifty days at least after the time appointed for the meeting thereof, unless it be by assent of his Majesty, his heirs or successors, *and* [my italics] of both Houses of Parliament assembled.

(*Source: Statutes of the Realm*, 16 Charles I, chapter 1)

With the Triennial Act passed and more reforms to come in 1641 (ship money and other taxes were declared illegal; no future royal minister could use a "royal" court such as Star Chamber for prosecutions) there appeared to be reasonable grounds for a settlement between Charles I and the Long Parliament. This seemed more likely in the spring of 1641, when four new Privy Councillors were appointed to widen Charles's support. Also, Oliver St John, Hampden's chief solicitor, was offered the post of Solicitorship, an important legal office in the government. It was widely expected that the King would appoint some of his leading opponents to key financial offices; the Earl of Bedford was thought to be in line for the post of Lord Treasurer, while John Pym would become Chancellor of the Exchequer. However, the death of Bedford meant that none of this happened.

### The Earl of Bedford:

The Earl of Bedford was a moderate who, according to Clarendon, might have helped bring about a settlement between King and Parliament, had he not died in May 1641:

The Earl of Bedford was a wise man, and of too great and plentiful a fortune to wish a subversion of the government, and it quickly appeared that he only intended to make himself and his friends great at court, not at all to lessen the court itself. . . . The Earl of Bedford secretly undertook to his majesty, that the Earl of Strafford's life should be preserved; and to procure his revenue to be settled as amply as any of his progenitors; the which he intended so really, that to my knowledge, he had it in design to endeavour the setting up of the excise in England, as the only natural means to advance the king's profit. He fell sick within a week after the bill of attainder [against Strafford] and died shortly afterwards.

(*Source: Clarendon Selections*, p. 133, OUP, 1953)

### The abolition of bishops:

There were other factors, in addition to the death of the moderate Earl of Bedford, that were working against a compromise between the King and Parliament. Partly reacting to pressures from outside Parliament, such as the petitions sent from cities and counties, some M.P.s were taking up a radical religious position. The Petition of the City of London requested the abolition of bishops. The more extreme Puritans, the Presbyterians, had been advocating the abolition of bishops since Elizabeth's reign, but until 1640 there had been little support for this policy. In May 1641 a group of radicals in the House of Commons, including Sir Harry Vane, Oliver Cromwell and Sir Edward Dering, presented a Bill to get rid of bishops "Root and Branch". In a speech of 12 June 1641 Vane argued that the government of the Church by bishops was "rotten and corrupt from the very foundation of it to the top". Some in the House of Commons supported this request for the abolition of bishops but many M.P.s found the proposal too radical and dangerous. Already in February 1641 Lord Digby had reacted with great concern to the petitions advocating the abolition of bishops:

There is no man within these walls more sensible of the heavy grievance of Church government than myself, nor whose affections are keener to

Of God,     Of Man,     Of the Divell.

*Only a small minority of Puritans, the Presbyterian group, advocated the abolition of bishops in the early seventeenth century. But with the calling of the Long Parliament a party emerged that wanted bishops eliminated from the English Church. Many pamphlets and broadsides were issued in support of the campaign for abolition. Here the bishop designated "of the Devil" is a Laudian bishop who is, according to the Puritans, following the road to superstition (and therefore nearly Catholic). He is therefore worse than the bishop "of man" who is at least following the ordinary Anglican Prayer Book. However, both bishops are inferior to the godly Puritan following the Bible.*

the clipping of these wings of the prelates whereby they have mounted to such insolencies. . . . But having reason to believe that some aim at a total extirpation [abolition] of bishops, which is against my heart . . . I cannot restrain myself from labouring to divert it.

(*Source: The Third Speech of Lord George Digby to the House of Commons concerning Bishops*, 1641, p. 17)

A few months later Sir Benjamin Rudyerd also expressed his concern:

But sir, one thing doth exceedingly trouble me. It turns me round about, it makes my whole reason vertiginous: which is, that so many do believe, against the wisdom of all ages, that now there can be no reformation without destruction; as if every sick body must be presently knocked on the head as past hope of care. . . . I am as much for reformation, for paying and maintaining religion as any man whatsoever, but I professe I am not for innovation, demolition nor abolition.

(*Source:* British Library, Tanner Manuscript, 66 folio, 184)

### The trial of the Earl of Strafford:

The death of the Earl of Bedford meant that the trial of Strafford in the House of Lords was sure to go ahead. Strafford was in fact found guilty of treason in the same month, May 1641, as the abolition of bishops was proposed. These two events coming together were an indication of how extreme the Parliament was becoming by the middle of 1641. Clarendon gives us a description of what happened when the Bill accusing Strafford of treason, which carried the death penalty, was put before the House of Lords:

> The next day great multitudes of people came down to Westminster, and crowded about the house of peers and exclaiming with great outcries 'that they would have justice . . .' and as any lord passed by, called 'Justice, justice' and with great rudeness and insolence pressing upon, and thrusting those lords whom they suspected not to favour that bill. . . . This unheard of act of insolence and sedition continued so many days till many happy lords grew so really apprehensive of having their brains beaten out, that they absented themselves from the house; and others changed their minds; and so in an afternoon, when of the fourscore who had been present at the trial, there were only six and forty lords in the house (the good people still crying at the doors for justice) they put the bill to the question, and eleven lords only dissenting, it passed that house. . .

(*Source: Clarendon Selections*, Oxford University Press, 1953, p. 142-143)

Strafford was executed on 12 May 1641 at Tower Hill. "I thank God," he said, "I am no more afraid of death . . . but do chearefully put off my dublet at this time, as ever I did when I went to bed."

*The importance of the execution of the Earl of Strafford can be seen from the crowds that the event attracted. Executions of any kind were considered to be a good spectator sport, but the execution of a royal minister was special – particularly in the London of 1641 where the mob was playing an increasingly important role. The fact that this print has been circulated in Germany shows that the event was of international importance.*

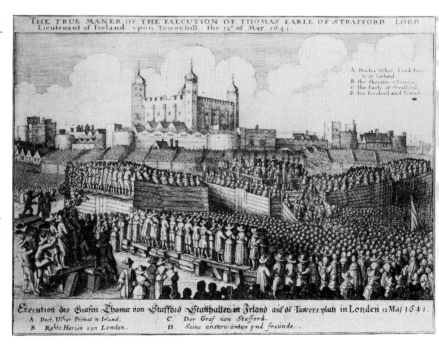

### The role of Pym and the London mob:

More than others, John Pym had been behind the execution of Strafford. Strafford was feared, lest he bring to English government the high-handed methods he used in Ireland as the King's deputy, but also because it was widely believed that he was prepared to accuse many of the leaders of the opposition of treason, for negotiating with the Scots – who were at war with England. The struggle between Pym and Strafford was perhaps one of basic survival. Moreover the London mob had played a significant part in the execution of Strafford; the mob was increasingly associated with Pym and radical political and religious policies as 1641 progressed:

The first outbursts in the early summer of 1640 had been unorganised and unco-ordinated. This, however, did not make them any less alarming, for apprentices were joined by large numbers drawn from the metropolitan proletariat, and notably the leather workers of Southwark and Bermondsey in an attempted assault on the Primate [the Archbishop of Canterbury] William Laud at Lambeth on 11 May...

Over the next few months the London mob was to become a formidable instrument in the hands of the radical group in the House of Commons. Pym and his associates organised mass petitions, intimidation was practised on people to make them sign, and fraudulent means were employed to obtain signatures to petitions which were often quite different to those which were finally presented.

(*Source:* R. Ashton, *The English Civil War*, Weidenfeld and Nicolson, 1978, p. 149)

---

*THINGS TO DO AND THINK ABOUT:*

*Putting together all the sources from pages 43-49, do you think they suggest that perhaps Clarendon is being too simplistic in seeing the death of Bedford as the main factor preventing a settlement? Weigh up the evidence in full in reaching your judgement.*

---

**THE IRISH REBELLION** Ever since the Short Parliament Pym had used anti-Catholic scare stories to maintain popular hatred of the King and his government. Charles himself had provided ammunition by negotiating with Catholic Spain in 1639; his Catholic wife Henrietta Maria had raised money abroad for the Royalists – which was considered almost treasonous – and there were prominent Catholics in the royal army. On 1 November 1641 news broke of the Irish Rebellion. It was an uprising of Irish Catholics hoping to seize power and thereafter to negotiate a better deal for the Catholic population. Though Ireland had a Catholic majority, its government was in the hands of Protestants; moreover, since the early seventeenth century much Irish land had been given to English and Scottish Protestant settlers, with a further decrease in Catholic power. The Catholic leaders, however, soon lost control of the rising and a general massacre ensued. Probably 4,000 Protestants were killed, with another 8,000 ejected from their homes in winter.

The Irish Rebellion had two major effects in England. Firstly, troops had to be raised to quell the Irish troubles, and this brought up all the old suspicions of whether the King could be entrusted with an army – or whether such an army might ultimately be used against Parliament. Secondly, the massacre of Protestants in Ireland seemed to confirm to English Protestants the evil nature of Catholicism and raised anew the fears which Pym in particular had skilfully used since the Short Parliament.

Representation of the principal Scenes in the bloody

IRISH MASSACRE in 1642 wherein 40000 PROTESTANTS

were inhumanly sacrificed by the papists.

*Propaganda like this, showing horrific tortures of Protestants in Ireland, including women and children, stirred the passions of English Protestants. Pym used the events in Ireland to keep the anti-Catholic feeling at as high a level as possible.*

## THE GRAND REMONSTRANCE

The Irish Rebellion so heightened passions and fears in the Long Parliament that when the Grand Remonstrance was presented in December 1641 it split the House of Commons down the middle. The Remonstrance was a general catalogue of the King's misrule, and suggestions for reform, but with a strong emphasis on the evils of popery and Arminianism. It was meant to appeal to the people of London and elsewhere as well as to M.P.s, since it was printed and circulated. It was passed by 159 votes to 148. For many M.P.s the Grand Remonstrance was a turning point; Sir Edward Dering, Geoffrey Palmer and Sir Ralph Hopton, all opponents of the Court up to this point, now became royalists.

## The Preamble to the Grand Remonstrance:

The Commons accused the papists, the bishops and the corrupt part of the clergy, and some of the King's councillors, of a plot to subvert the fundamental laws of the kingdom. They then described their methods:

First to maintain continual differences and discontents between the king and the people, upon questions of prerogative and liberty, that so they might have the advantage of siding with him, and under the notions of men addicted to his service, gain to themselves and their parties the place of greatest trust and power in the kingdom.

[The aim of royal government was] to introduce and countenance such opinions and ceremonies as are fittest for accommodation with Popery, to increase and maintain ignorance, looseness and profaneness in the people; that those of three parties, Papists, Arminians and Libertines they might compose a body fit to act such counsels and resolutions as were most conducible to their own ends.

(*Source:* J. Rushworth, *Historical Collections, 1659,* Vol. 4)

## Sir Edward Dering:

This Remonstrance is now in progress upon its last foot in this House; I must give a vote unto it, one way or another. My conscience bids me not to dare to be affirmative; sings the bird in my breast and I do cheerfully believe the tune to be good. . . . I did not dream that we should remonstrate downwards, tell stories to the people and talk of the king as of a third person.

The use and end of such Remonstrance I understand not; at least I hope I do not.

(*Source:* J. Rushworth, *Historical Collections, 1659,* vol. 4, p. 425, 1721 edition)

Sir John Colpepper, another former opponent of the King, who joined the Court in late 1641, was appalled by the appeal to the people: they would realize that

all this was done by them, but not for them and grow weary of the journey-work and set up for themselves [i.e. get tired of acting for the likes of Pym and seize power themselves], call parity and independence, liberty . . . destroy all rights and properties, all extinctions of families and merit, and by this means the splendid and exultantly distinguished form of government end in a dark, equal chaos of confusion, and the long line of our many noble ancestors in a Jack Cade or a Wat Tyler [both leaders of Peasant Rebellions].

(*Source:* quoted in Sir Simon D'Ewes' diary, p. 187, 1942 edition)

**THE KING THROWS AWAY HIS CHANCE OF RALLYING MODERATE OPINION**

Charles I gained considerable support as a result of a moderate reply to the Grand Remonstrance. But the King lacked political skills throughout the whole crisis and he undid much of his good work over the Remonstrance with the tactless appointment of the unpopular Cavalier Lunsford as Lieutenant of the Tower of London. Humiliatingly, Charles bowed to public protest and demonstration by dismissing him after only three days. The King lost a further opportunity of winning over more moderates by his attempted arrest of Pym and four fellow M.P.s in January 1642.

The King came, with all his guard, and two or three hundred soldiers and gentlemen. The King commanded the soldiers to stay in the hall and sent us word he was at the door. . . . Then the King came upward towards the chair [of the Speaker]. . . . After he had looked a great while, he told us he would not break our privileges but treason had no privilege; he came for those five gentlemen. . . . Then he called for Mr. Pym and Mr. Holles

*Charles I's entering Parliament with his bodyguard to demand the arrest of five M.P.s, including Pym, who had attacked him so much, was considered a grave breach of Parliamentary privilege. This action brought open conflict between the King and Parliament one step closer.*

by name, but no answer was made. Then he asked the Speaker if they were here, or where they were. Upon that, the Speaker fell on his knees and desired his excuse, for he was a servant to the House, and had neither eyes, nor tongue to see or to say anything but what they had commanded him. Then the King told him that he thought his own eyes were as good as his, and then said his birds were flown, but he did expect the House would send them to him. . .

(*Source:* J. Rushworth, *Historical Collections, 1659*, vol. 4, p. 478)

There was a drift towards civil war from January 1642. The zealots on either side may have waited eagerly for engagement, but over most of the country, and even among many M.P.s, the reaction was one of great despondency.

## Sir Thomas Knyvett to his wife, 18 May 1642:

I cannot let any opportunitye pass of telling the howe I doe; I prayse Allmighty God that I am at this present as well I was these 7 yeers. I would to God I could write thee good any newes, but that is impossible so long as the spirit of contradiction rainges between King and Parliament higher still than ever, And tis to be feared this thretning storme will not bee allayed without some showers (I praye not a deluge) of bloode. The one party nowe growes as resolute as the other is obstinate. . . . Oh sweete harte, I am nowe in a great stayght what to doe. Walking this other morning at Westminster, Sir John Potts, with commissary Maltford saluted me with a commission from the Lord of Warwicke to take upon me (by vertue of an Ordinance of Parliament) my Company. . . . I had not received this many hours, but I met with a declaration poknt Blanck against it by the King. This distraction made me to advise with some understanding men what condition I do stand in, which is no other than a great many men of Quality doe.

(*Source:* The Knyvett Letters 1620-1644, ed. B. Schofield, 1949)

# Taking Sides

*Charles I sets up his standard near Nottingham, 1642. This was in effect the official declaration by the King that he was at war with some of his subjects. Note that in his declaration he undertakes to protect the privileges of Parliament. Conversely, those who supported Parliament professed to be doing so in the interests of the monarchy as well.*

By the time Charles tried to arrest the five M.P.s the political situation was deteriorating rapidly. The House of Commons was expecting violence – on 30 December 1641 M.P.s' servants were ordered to bring pistols to defend the House. By 10 January 1642 the King was so afraid of mob assault that he left London, never to return until 1648 to face his trial and subsequent execution. Already the King was contemplating the possibility of an armed clash between himself and Parliament. In mid-January his supporters tried unsuccessfully to seize the huge collection of weapons kept at Hull. Both the King and Parliament increased their propaganda trying to convince the country of the rightness of their respective policies. Many local petitions however continued to plead for the King and Parliament to settle their differences. By the middle of August Charles had made up his mind. There must be an immediate trial of strength. By 22 August, with the King unfurling his standard at Nottingham, the war had effectively begun. Despite the outbreak of hostilities, even in 1642 Parliament believed in the theory of King and Parliament working together.

The Kings Declaration to his Gentry & Army September 1642.

*The King after setting up his Standard, drew his Men to a Rendezvous, and then caused his military Orders to be read, and in a set Speech declared the Confidence he had in them, solemnly engagd himself to preserve the Liberty & Property of the Subject, and if his Arms were blest to govern according to the known laws & to maintain the Privilege of Parliaments, and that when he willingly faild in these particulars he would expect no Relief from Man nor Protection from Heaven.*

**SEVENTEENTH-CENTURY VIEWS** The matter with us [i.e. the nation], is quite and generally mistaken, and the question altogether wrongly stated viz. 'Whether we should obey King or parliament?' For the King and parliament are not like two parallel lines which can never meet, nor like two incompatible qualities, which cannot be both in one subject. . . . For by siding with parliament, in those things which are according to law, we side with and serve with the king.

(*Source:* Historical Manuscript Commission, Portland Manuscript, vol. 1, p. 90)

Jonathan Langley from Shropshire could not see any great religious divide, and wanted to be left in peace:

and [for my part] my conscience tells me they both intend the Protestant Religion what reason have I therefore to fall out with either . . . to live at Home is my earnest desire, beseeching you that no more protestations be urged upon me, for I find in my own Conscience I have sufficiency enough of this, nor to be compelled to bear Arms, nor clapt up as disaffected to his Majesty, which very word I abhor from my heart.

(*Source: Neutrality is Malignancy*, 1648, p. 8)

The issues between King and Parliament were not absolutely clear-cut. You have already seen (pages, 9, 53 and above), also, that some people tried to remain neutral. The transformation from conflict between Parliament and the King to the outbreak of fighting was caused by activists on either side. What motivated such activities? Why did people take sides in the Civil War?

## Clarendon's view on Somerset:

For though the gentlemen of ancient families and estates in that county were for the most part well affected to the King, and easily discerned by what faction the Parliament was governed, yet there were a people of inferior degree who, by good husbandry, clothing and other thriving arts had gotten very great fortunes, and by degrees getting themselves into the gentlemen's estates, were angry that they found not themselves in the same esteem and reputation with those whose estates they had; . . . these from the beginning were fast friends to the Parliament.

(*Source:* Clarendon, *History of the Great Rebellion*, II, p. 296)

## Clarendon's view on Lancashire and Cheshire:

The town of Manchester had from the beginning (out of that factious humour which possessed most corporations and the pride of their wealth) opposed the King and declared magisterially for Parliament. But as the majority part of the county consisted of Papists . . . so it was believed that there was not one man of ten throughout that province who meant not to be dutiful to the King.

(*Source:* Clarendon, *History of the Great Rebellion*, II, p. 472)

## Richard Baxter's view:

On the Parliament's side were (besides themselves) the smaller part, as some thought, of the gentry in most of the counties and the greatest part of the tradesmen and freeholders, and the middle sort of men, especially in those corporations and counties which depended on clothing and such manufactures. . . . If you ask the reasons of this difference, ask also why in France it is not commonly the nobility nor the beggars, but the merchants and the middle sort of men that were Protestant. . .

(*Source: Reliquiat Baxterianat*, 1696, p. 30-1)

## TWENTIETH-CENTURY VIEWS

Two modern historians have reached very positive conclusions on the reasons for taking sides:

### Lawrence Stone:

Far more decisive than any socio-economic correlations is that with religion. In Yorkshire over one third of the Royalist gentry were Catholics, and over half of the Parliamentarians were Puritan. To put it another way, of those who took sides, 90% of all Catholics became Royalists and 72% of all Puritans became Parliamentarians. *All* the Parliamentary leaders in Yorkshire had a previous record of strong Puritan sympathies.

(*Source:* Lawrence Stone, *The Causes of the English Revolution*, Routledge and Kegan Paul, 1972)

### John Morrill:

If there were profound differences between the two sides they were over religion. In 1642-43 almost all those who can be found committed to (as against going along with) the King were either Catholic recusants or strong upholders of episcopacy (bishops). . . On the Parliamentarian side can be found almost all those who campaigned against bishops and a great many who, while they were prepared to argue for a modified episcopacy, saw the structure of Church government as optional and negotiable. More generally, there was an obsessive anti-Catholicism among most Parliamentarians nurtured over decades in the struggle against Spain and the Jesuits, and now increasingly focused on the Court itself. . .

(*Source:* John Morrill, *Reactions to the Civil War*, Macmillan, 1982)

---

*THINGS TO DO AND THINK ABOUT:*

*How do the seventeenth-century sources differ from the twentieth-century ones in their reasons for people taking sides?*

*Can we rely more on primary sources than on secondary sources?*

*Look again at Clarendon on Lancashire and Cheshire, and at Richard Baxter. In what ways do these suggest that in fact they might agree, at least to some extent, with the secondary sources?*

---

# The Finale:
# the Execution of the King, 1649

One problem facing historians is that events seldom have a clean finish in history. In many respects the culmination of the English Civil War is the execution of Charles I in 1649. But even when you have managed to explain why people took sides, you are a long way from explaining why the finale of the King's execution took place. No one, or practically no one in 1642 wanted to abolish monarchy: what, therefore, caused the change?

**RELIGIOUS UPHEAVALS**

The war led to great religious upheavals. By 1644 the Anglican Church had been virtually abolished. This gave individuals a freedom they had never enjoyed before – a freedom to choose their religion. As a result, separate Churches sprang up and radical Puritanism spread. Many clergy who had previously served the Anglican Church lost their jobs; in all, about 28% of all clergy were ejected from office in the 1640s and 1650s. In the East of England the ejection of ministers was done by the local "Committee for Scandalous Ministers"; in other parts of the country it was done by Parliament's "Committee for Plundered Ministers" meeting in London.

*The more extreme Puritans had always objected to the use of crosses and crucifixes. Once the Civil War was started the Puritans became increasingly powerful within London, and here we see them demolishing a cross in Cheapside. This was only one of a number of pieces of sculpture or church furnishings which the Puritans demolished because they considered such things to be "popish".*

**Articles against Edward Barton, Rector of Grundisburgh, Suffolk, 1 April 1644:**

1.  Mr. Barton hath not continued at his living since he came to be parson of that parish, but hath heretofore come thither once or twice in a year for a week or a fortnight to receive the profits of the living. . .
4.  Mr. Barton doth constantly read his sermons which he performs very imperfectly and doth not usually exceed the space of half an hour.

a Confectioner · a Smith · a Sho=maker · a Taylor
a Sadler · a Porter · a Box-maker · a Sope-boyler
a Glover · a Meal-man · a Chicken-man · a Button-maker

**Information against Mr Ryley of Newton Sidney, Wiltshire, by Anne Holdway, 2 May 1646:**

1. That he neglected the Wednesday Fast appointed by the Parliament and observed the Friday Fast (appointed by the King.)
2. . . . He is a common swearer and common gamester and a frequenter of taverns. . .
3. He discountenanced preaching. . .
4. He pressed the people to observe the ceremonies . . . caused the place where the Table [the Communion Table] stood to be raised.
5. He extolled the Book of Common Prayer . . . [he said] that laymen ought not to meddle with the Scripture and that women ought not to read the Scriptures.

*Why do you think the radical Puritans who were increasingly influential in the Parliamentary ranks objected to the points mentioned?*

## POLITICAL UPHEAVALS

*By 1647 the politically radical "Leveller" movement was making itself felt, especially in [L]ondon and in the Army. Their opponents argued that their programme, [es]pecially on the extension of voting rights to most men, would mean that [En]gland would be governed by the tradesmen shown here.*

Since the Church had always played a crucial role in politics, the disintegration of the National Church had an important political impact. There was a desire for greater political freedoms and by 1647 a group called the Levellers put forward a democratic programme, including a demand for "one man one vote" (excluding servants) which would have been unthinkable at the beginning of the seventeenth century. But perhaps the most important consequence of the war was the creation of a permanent Standing Army, the New Model Army. By 1647 the New Model Army, in which Oliver Cromwell was very powerful, was a strong political force, ready to challenge Parliament over certain issues. This New Model Army also tended to be a breeding ground for political and religious extremism; it was very unlike any English army before or since. It was the army that finally decided the fate of King Charles I. After the King had raised a military force in Scotland and provoked another Civil War in 1648 to try to regain the kingdom, the army took a vote that Charles should be brought to trial. In December 1648 one of their number, Colonel Pride, asked M.P.s as they entered Parliament whether *they* would support the idea of the King's trial. Those who opposed the idea were excluded; it was the remainder or the "Rump" Parliament that finally found Charles I guilty of "breaking his contract" to the people. Charles refused to plead to such charges and he was found guilty by default.

## THE EXECUTION OF THE KING

So on 30 January 1649 one of the most momentous events of the seventeenth century took place. Charles I was executed outside the Banqueting Hall in London. The execution is described by an eyewitness:

On the day of his execution, which was Tuesday Jan. 30th, I stood amongst the crowd in the street before Whitehall gate, where the scaffold was erected . . . the blow I saw given, and can truly say with a sad heart; at the instant whereof I remember well, there was such a groan by the thousands then present, as I never heard before and desire I may never hear again. There was according to order one Troop immediately marching from Charing Cross to Westminster and another from Westminster to Charing Cross purposely to muster the people, and to disperse and scatter them so that I had so much ado amongst the rest to escape home without hurt.

(*Source:* Diaries and Letters of Philip Henry and M.H. Lee, published 1682)

## CONCLUSION

Even months before the King's death few would have envisaged such a momentous event. Eleven years later, his son Charles II was welcomed back to England. What causes events to move so swiftly? One of the problems you have in looking at cause and motivation in history is that events often turn out in a way that the original instigators did not want or could not have predicted. Perhaps from 1637 and certainly from 1641, events in England had a momentum of their own that few individuals had consciously sought. The explanation may be that the English Civil War was started by the ruling classes, but completed by "the people". The disintegration of traditional authority led to a sense of permanent crisis.

# Sources

James Harrington (1611-77), **The Commonwealth of Oceana**, 1656
This was one of the major seventeenth-century interpretations of the English Civil War. *Oceana* was intended to place the Civil War in its historical perspective, and Harrington was convinced that the main key to events in the seventeenth century was the economic one. Harrington was particularly used by modern historians such as R.H. Tawney to give a social and economic interpretation to the Civil War. The social and economic emphasis is a little less prominent today than it was in the 1950s and 1960s, but Harrington remains an important and respected source.

Earl of Clarendon, **History of the Rebellion and Civil Wars in England (1702-4)**
Clarendon's work was the first full-length treatment of the Civil War and events leading up to it. In 1906 it was described by A.J. Grant as "epoch-making in the development of English historical writing". More recently, Christopher Hill has written, "Whatever his defects as a politician, Clarendon was a great historian". Clarendon set out to produce a balanced and impartial view of events in England up to and including the Civil War, aiming "to do justice to every man who hath fallen into the quarrel in which side soever". Though ultimately a leading Royalist (see biography), Clarendon was not uncritical of Charles I, and he was even more critical of the actions of Queen Henrietta Maria, Charles's wife. He was reasonably kind if not enthusiastic in his judgements on Laud and Strafford. He was less impartial in dealing with Parliamentarians, writing of John Hampden that he "was a man of much great cunning". Overall, however, Clarendon's history is balanced and reliable.

Another major and valuable source which first appeared in the 1650s was the **Historical Collections of John Rushworth** (1612-90). Rushworth had a clear historical method: he wanted to relate the events without interpretation. "I pretend only in this work to a bare narrative of matter of fact digested in order of time, not interposing my own opinion or interpretation of actions". Certainly, Rushworth's accounts are strong on fact and detail, with little obvious personal interpretation. If modern historians have found Rushworth fairly reliable and objective, this was not the seventeenth-century reaction. Since he served as secretary to Oliver Cromwell in the 1650s, his work was vigorously attacked by Royalists in the Restoration period (1660-88).

**Parliamentary sources**
**The Statutes of the Realm** (for the sixteenth and seventeenth centuries) tell us about new Acts of Parliament such as the Triennial Act 1641, giving all the details of the provisions of these new laws. But the Statutes give no information about how an Act came into being and the debates that preceded it. By contrast, the **Lords Journal** and the **Commons Journal**, products of sixteenth-century development, tell us about the views of those respective Houses. The greatest detail about debate and controversy within Parliament comes from the diaries of M.P.s such as Sir Simon D'Ewes. Such parliamentary diaries give a wealth of detail about individual positions on particular issues, though of course the personal views of the diarist have to be borne in mind. In D'Ewes's case it has to be remembered that he is a Puritan.

**Religious sources**
These sources are most likely to be written from a particular viewpoint. They vary greatly too: from the

one-thousand-page book of William Prynne – *Histriomatrix* (see biography) to the *London Petition* of 1641, advocating the abolition of bishops. There are also personal works, and parts of Ralph Josselin's diary tell us much about the Puritan religion.

**Diaries and letters**
With the increase in literacy in the seventeenth century both these sources increased considerably. They allow us a much greater insight into people than is possible for earlier centuries. Diaries such as Ralph Josselin's mentioned above tell us not only about religion but about the everyday preoccupations of a clergyman who lived through the Civil War, while Henry Townshend's diary gives a vivid picture of the hardships and trials of the Civil War. We get some particularly good letters from M.P.s or other gentlemen doing business in London, to their wives back home. Letters from the likes of Thomas Knyvett, which span a period from 1629-42, are especially valuable.

**Modern publications**
Books on the English Civil War have to give emphasis to one interpretation or another. Christopher Hill's *Puritanism and Revolution* (Secker and Warburg, 1958) gives prominence to the rise of Puritanism but sees this linked to longer-term economic factors. Puritanism is linked to the rise of more commercial attitudes and Hill is sympathetic to many of Harrington's ideas. Lawrence Stone in *The Causes of the English Revolution 1529-1642* (Routledge and Kegan Paul, 1972) shows his belief in long-term social and economic factors in starting his book in 1529. But he also stresses the short-term political developments, and tries to place the English Civil War in the context of other "revolutions" outside of

England. J.S. Morrill's *The Revolt of the Provinces* (Longman, 1980) stresses the importance of religion in the outbreak of the Civil War, but also argues that a significant number of Englishmen (and women) wanted to remain neutral. The most recent general work on the period which gives a balanced and incisive summary of recent interpretations of the Civil War is Derek Hirst's *Authority and Conflict in England 1603-58* (Edward Arnold, 1986).

## Local Sources

| | |
|---|---|
| J.S. Morrill | *Cheshire 1630-1660* (1974) |
| M. Coate | *Cornwall in the Great Civil War and Interregnum* (1930) |
| E. Andriette | *Devon and Exeter in the Civil War* (1972) |
| C. Holmes | *The Eastern Association* (1974) |
| G.H. Goodwin | *The Civil War in Hampshire* (1882) |
| A.M. Everitt | *The Community of Kent and the Great Rebellion* (1966) |
| E. Broxap | *The Great Civil War in Lancashire 1642-51* (1910) |
| R.W. Kretton-Cremer | *Norfolk in the Civil War* (1969) |
| A.C. Wood | *Nottinghamshire in the Civil War* (1937) |
| A.L. Leach | *The History of the Civil War in Pembrokeshire and on its Borders* (1937) |
| W.J. Farrow | *The Great Civil War in Shropshire: 1642-49* (1926) |
| D.E. Underdown | *Somerset in the Civil Wars and Interregnum* (1973) |
| A. Everitt | *Suffolk and the Great Rebellion* (Suffolk Record Society, 1961) |
| A. Fletcher | *A Country Community in Peace and War: Sussex 1600-1660* (1975) |
| J.R. Philipps | *The Civil War in Wales and the Marches* (2 vols, 1874) |
| J.W. Willis-Bund | *The Civil War in Worcestershire 1642-46* (1905) |

Ask at your local library or local record offices, for these or other similar works.

# Biographies

## BUCKINGHAM, George Villiers, Duke of (1592-1628)

Born in Leicestershire, he first met James I in 1614 where the King was supposedly impressed by "his sprightly youth". He became a member of the King's household in 1615, and was created Viscount Villiers and Baron Waddon in 1616. Already a rising political figure he was created Marquis of Buckingham in 1618, a firm favourite of James I, and probably the most important man at Court. In 1623 Buckingham went to Spain with Prince Charles (the future Charles I) to finalize a Spanish marriage for the Prince. Though the marriage never materialized he established a good relationship with Charles so that on the King's accession in 1625 Buckingham if anything increased his power. He was in charge of English foreign policy from 1625 to 1628. He was heavily criticized for its lack of success, and the object of much hatred because of his dominance at Court. On 23 August 1628 he was assassinated by John Felton at Portsmouth (see page 33).

## CLARENDON Edward Hyde, 1st Earl of (1609-74)

He was a member of the Long Parliament. At first he joined in the general attack on Charles I's politics, and even supported the trial of the Earl of Strafford (see below). But he was not a Puritan, and he certainly opposed the attack on bishops. He also grew worried that Pym's tactics (see below) in the Long Parliament would lead to disorder. He gradually changed his position and before the end of 1641 he was a staunch supporter of the King. He spent many years in exile after the defeat of the Royalists, but he became Charles II's leading minister after 1660. He was dismissed in 1667 and spent the rest of his life in exile, mainly in France. He is most famous for his

*History of the Great Rebellion*, as he called the English Civil War, which was first published in Oxford in 1702-4.

### ELIOT Sir John (1592-1632)

He was born in Cornwall. He was originally a friend of the Duke of Buckingham. He first sat for Parliament in 1624 where other M.P.s were impressed by his oratory. In the 1624 Parliament Eliot supported Buckingham's policy of war against Spain. By 1626, however, Eliot had turned against Buckingham and the King, following the failure of Buckingham's expedition to Cadiz against Spain. In that year Eliot led a furious Parliamentary attack on Buckingham and also argued that Parliament should not vote taxes for the King until he dismissed Buckingham. In 1627 Eliot was imprisoned in the Gatehouse, London, for refusing to pay the Forced Loan which Charles I had levied once Parliament refused to vote him taxes. He supported the Petition of Right in 1628 and he also attacked the King's religious policies. In 1629, after disorders in Parliament, he was again imprisoned in the Tower, where he died.

### HAMPDEN John (1594-1643)

He lived in Great Hampden, Bucks. He sat in the Parliaments of the 1620s and he was a friend of Eliot, with whom he corresponded in the Tower in the years 1629-32, while watching over the education of Eliot's children. He owes his reputation to his opposition to Ship Money. Hampden challenged the King's right to levy this tax, and though the Exchequer Judges voted by 7 to 5 in favour of the King, Clarendon wrote that the judgement "proved of more advantage and credit to the gentleman condemned than to the King's service". Hampden sat in the Short Parliament of 1640 and the Long Parliament. He played an active though not prominent part in the trial of Strafford.

### LAUD William (1573-1645)

He was born at Reading, son of a clothier. He went to St John's College, Oxford, where he was influenced by John Buckeridge against the Calvinist faith, so dominant in the Church of England by the seventeenth century. In 1611 Laud became President of St John's, just about the time that there was a reaction against Calvinism in Holland, led by a person named Arminius. Laud became influential in the English Church on the accession of Charles I in 1625, and he immediately promoted Arminianism (see glossary), a name taken from the Dutch Arminius. This movement aimed to make the Church of England much less Calvinist. In 1628 Laud became Bishop of London, and in 1633 Archbishop of Canterbury. He was a Privy Councillor in the 1630s, and closely associated with the Personal Rule of Charles I. He led a vigorous attack on the Puritans in the 1630s and punished three of them, Prynne, Bastwick and Burton, savagely, for their attack on his Church policies. He was immediately imprisoned by the Long Parliament for his part in the Personal Rule. In January 1645 he was finally executed when the House of Commons decided that he had attempted to alter the foundations of the Church and the state and this was treasonous.

### PRYNNE William (1600-69)

Educated at Bath Grammar School and Oriel College, Oxford, he was a lawyer, a member of Lincoln's Inn, and a militant Puritan. In 1632 Prynne published a book called *Histriomatrix* which consists of over 1,000 pages showing that stage plays (of the kind performed at Court) were incentives to immorality and against the scriptures. He was particularly offensive about actresses, and this was taken as a gross insult to Henrietta Maria, wife of Charles I, who had acted in Court plays. For this and his attack on Laud's religious policies he was brought before the Court of the Star Chamber in 1634, and he eventually suffered the fate of being sentenced to lose his ears, pay £5,000 and be imprisoned for life. He was released by the Long Parliament.

### PYM John (1584-1643)

He came from Bridgwater in Somerset. He entered the House of Commons in 1614 and sat for all the Parliaments up to the Long Parliament. He played an important part in the key issues in Parliament from 1625 to 1629. He was in favour of voting the King adequate taxes to fight the war against Spain (unlike Eliot – see above) but he was particularly opposed to Laud and Arminianism (see above). Pym was probably the most important politician in the House of Commons in the years 1640-43, opposing Charles I on many issues. He used the London mob to stir up anti-Catholic feeling, and was largely responsible for the trial of the Earl of Strafford (see page 47). He was also responsible for the Grand Remonstrance in November 1641 (see page 50). He masterminded an alliance between Parliament and the Scots in 1643, but did not live long enough to see the fruits of this in the Parliamentary victory against the King.

### STRAFFORD Thomas Wentworth, Earl of (1593-1641)

Educated at St John's College, Cambridge, he sat in the 1614 Parliament as M.P. for Yorkshire. He was in the House of Commons again in the 1620s, where he was one of the most outspoken critics of the King. He opposed the Forced Loan of 1627, but in 1628 he was appointed to a royal office, President of the Council of the North. From that point onwards Wentworth became a fervent supporter of the King. In 1632 he was appointed Lord Deputy of Ireland, where he acquired a reputation as a strong, tough ruler. Though he had little direct influence on the Personal Rule of Charles I in the 1630s, since he was in Ireland, the King came to rely on his advice especially in the years 1638-40 at the time of the Scottish Crisis. He was the one royal advisor who was really feared by the Parliamentarians. This accounts for Pym's determination to destroy him. He was condemned by the House of Lords in May 1641 on the charge of treason (see page 47).

# Glossary

| | |
|---|---|
| **cavalier** | a supporter of the King in the Civil War. |
| **coate and conduct money** | a tax levied specifically to raise troops for a particular campaign. |
| **delinquent** | a term used by Parliamentarians about those who supported the King in the Civil War and were therefore liable to suffer confiscation of land or heavy fines. |
| **free quarter** | free provisions for troops. Communities and individuals were forced to provide these for troops billeted on them. |
| **Lower House** | House of Commons. |
| **magazine** | a collection of weapons. |
| **offices** | positions of power in the church or state. |
| **papist** | term used by Englishmen, especially Puritans, to describe Catholics. |
| **popery** | term used to describe Catholicism. |
| **predestination** | the belief that all men and women are "predetermined" to be saved or damned (i.e. go to heaven or hell) from the time they are born. This means that no man or woman can do anything to earn salvation; they cannot do anything on their own to get to heaven. Their salvation is purely in the hands of God. This was a central belief of all Puritans and most Anglicans before Arminianism challenged the belief in 1625. |
| **real wages** | wages adjusted for inflation. For example, if a labourer has the same wages as before but prices have risen, then his *real* wages have fallen. |
| **recusant** | a Catholic who refused to make even an occasional appearance at Anglican services. |
| **roundhead** | a supporter of the Parliamentary side in the Civil War. |
| **Star Chamber** | a court established by the King in the late fifteenth century and where no jury was used. The Chamber was often used by the Crown to enforce unpopular policies. |
| **Upper House** | House of Lords. |
| **wardship** | If a nobleman or great landowner died while his male heir was under twenty-one, the King had the right, as feudal overlord, to look after the heir until he was twenty-one years old. Frequently the King sold that "right of wardship" and it thus became a profitable source of income. |

# Date List

| | |
|---|---|
| **1603** | Accession of James I. |
| **1625** | Accession of Charles I. |
| | Arminianism begins to be promoted within Anglican Church. |
| **1629** | Charles I dismisses his third Parliament and decides to rule without Parliament. |
| **1637** | John Hampden challenges the King's right to levy ship money. |
| | Charles I tries to impose a new Laudian Prayer Book on Scotland – the beginnings of the Scottish Crisis. |
| **1640 November** | Charles forced to call Long Parliament to deal with mounting crises in the kingdom, especially the invasion of the Scots. |
| **1641 May** | Royal minister, Earl of Strafford, executed for treason. |
| **1641 November** | News of rebellion in Ireland. |
| | Grand Remonstrance. |
| **1642 January** | Charles I tries to arrest five leading opposition M.P.s in Parliament. |
| **1642 October** | Battle of Edgehill: the first proper battle of the Civil War. |
| **1644 July** | Battle of Marston Moor: the King effectively loses the North. |
| **1645 July** | Battle of Langport near Bridgwater: Royalist defeat effectively ends Civil War. |
| **1647 October** | Strength of political radicalism seen in the emergence of the Levellers. |
| **1648** | Second Civil War. |
| **1649 January 30** | King Charles I executed. |

# Index